Publication Number 706
AMERICAN LECTURE SERIES®

A Monograph in
The BANNERSTONE DIVISION of
AMERICAN LECTURES IN PHILOSOPHY

Edited by
MARVIN FARBER
State University of New York at Buffalo

EVIL AND THE CONCEPT OF GOD

By

EDWARD H. MADDEN

State University of New York at Buffalo

and

PETER H. HARE

State University of New York at Buffalo

CHARLES C THOMAS • PUBLISHER

Springfield • Illinois • U.S.A.

Published and Distributed Throughout the World by
CHARLES C THOMAS • PUBLISHER
BANNERSTONE HOUSE
301-327 East Lawrence Avenue, Springfield, Illinois, U.S.A.
NATCHEZ PLANTATION HOUSE
735 North Atlantic Boulevard, Fort Lauderdale, Florida, U.S.A.

With THOMAS BOOKS *careful attention is given to all details of manufacturing and design. It is the Publisher's desire to present books that are satisfactory as to their physical qualities and artistic possibilities and appropriate for their particular use.* THOMAS BOOKS *will be true to those laws of quality that assure a good name and good will.*

Printed in the United States of America
W-2

For
Marian and Daphne

CONTENTS

The following books have appeared thus far in this Series:

Chapter One

The Riddle of God and Evil

I

IT IS A NOTORIOUS fact that the very way a philosophical problem is formulated not only determines its possible answers but already reflects commitments. So we shall formulate the riddle of God and evil in a tentative way and comment on its structure as we proceed. One version of the riddle is this: If God is unlimited in power and goodness, why is there so much *prima facie* gratuitous evil in the world? If he is unlimited in power he should be able to remove unnecessary evil, and if he is unlimited in goodness he should want to remove it; but he does not. Apparently he is limited either in power or goodness, or does not exist at all. There have been numerous strategies advanced to avoid, eliminate, or solve this riddle but before these strategies can be fairly criticized it is crucial to become quite clear about the exact nature of the riddle.

It must be clear at the outset that the problem we raise is not why there is any evil at all in the world. Although the latter problem is a legitimate one and leads to interesting discussions about God's alleged ability or inability to create a perfect world, this problem is a sterile one in every other way since some evil obviously serves good ends.[1] But much evil resists simple explanation; it is *prima facie* gratuitous. The really interesting problem of evil is whether the apparent gratuity can be explained away by more ingenious measures or whether the gratuity is real and hence detrimental to religious belief.

It should also be clear that the problem we raise is not one of formal inconsistency.[2] We are *not* claiming that the following statements constitute an inconsistent set: God is almighty, God is all-knowing, God is infinitely good, and evil, created by this

3

being, exists in the finite world. To state the problem in this way begs the main question at issue, namely, whether or not the evil which is plainly evident is gratuitous or serves some purpose and ignores the fact that some evil obviously serves good ends which could not otherwise be achieved. The very possibility of stating the problem of evil as a formal contradiction depends upon claiming that 'There is no morally sufficient reason for an almighty God to allow any instances of evil' is necessarily true. In light of the above points such a claim would be absurd. Moreover, if the problem of evil were stated as a formal contradiction the theist would have no difficulty whatever in rebutting it.[3] He would not have to show even that there is a reasonable or probable explanation of evil. To rebut the alleged self-contradiction he only has to show that there is some *possible* explanation of evil, whether it take the form of saying that some higher good may be served or that any creation may entail the existence of some evil. That the present formulation of and answer to the problem of evil is not the central issue is well attested by the enormous amount of energy and ingenuity displayed by religious writers themselves in shaping and refining their answers to what they take to be a serious challenge.

While the problem of evil as we formulate it is not a question of formal inconsistency, the theist is sometimes straightforwardly inconsistent, we shall see, in trying to meet it. This problem arises when the only logically possible reasons for the existence of an evil are incompatible with the moral principles which the theist has previously claimed were sanctioned by God (or with the moral principles built into the very concept of God.)[4]

As soon as one formulates the problem of evil the question inevitably asked is, "How do you define *evil?*" To ask for a definition or analysis of *evil* seems like a promising move at first, but in fact turns out not to be. The point is this: Defining the notion of evil is irrelevant to the problem of evil we have posed because the problem remains unchanged for whatever definition is accepted. Suppose, for example, one accepts St. Augustine's definition of *evil* as "the privation of good." Evil has no being itself but is simply the absence of good. Being itself is always good, and evil occurs only as the corruption of a substance. The problem of evil still remains, however, because now one has the problem of explaining why, in the present world, there is so much *prima facie* gratuitous absence of good, so much apparently needless privation. Since the problem of evil will arise on any non-question-begging definition of *evil*, we shall not embark upon our own analysis of this term.

While a definition of *evil* is irrelevant to our problem, the specification of what is to count as evil is very relevant indeed. The problem is to specify examples of evil in a way that does not prejudice the question of gratuity. The safest way to achieve this goal, and the one frequently followed, is to draw only from the ordinary and common-sensical extension of evil, thereby avoiding the philosophical criteria of evil which have caused so much confusion in the past.[5] We follow this procedure throughout the book. Our examples of *prima facie* gratuitous evils are taken always from that whole set of undesirable experiences and deeds which all of us, minus our philosophical views, would prefer to avoid. This set includes, at a minimum, unbearable pain and suffering caused either by natural events or the acts of other men, character defects, immoral acts, physical and mental deformity, the prosperity of rogues, and the failure of honest men.

It might be objected, however, that we do not succeed in being unprejudiced by taking such a common-sensical view of what counts as evil. This view, it could be argued, misses the point that several theodicies reject, more or less completely, ordinary notions of good and evil. One version of the ultimate harmony view rejects them altogether and posits a "higher morality" of God in their stead, while other theodicies, depending upon "theological values" and "aesthetic values," reject large parts of the ordinary notions of evil. We will have numerous things to say about these claims in the proper places; suffice it to say now that any system of values which repudiates all ordinary judgments of good and evil runs the grave risk of being utterly vacuous. And in all cases where ordinary notions are rejected, whether wholly or in part, we attempt to show that the resulting theodicy, *granting its own view of values,* is inadequate.

The evils of life traditionally have been classified by philosophers into "physical" and "moral" ones.[6] This distinction has been made in various ways and none of them are faultless, but we shall salvage what we can of the distinction because it will serve a useful classificatory function later. *Physical evil,* we shall say, denotes the terrible pain, suffering, and untimely death caused by events like fire, flood, landslide, hurricane, earthquake, tidal wave, and famine/and by diseases like cancer, leprosy, and tetanus—as well as the crippling defects and deformities like blindness, deafness, dumbness, shrivelled limbs, and insanity by which so many sentient beings are cheated of the full benefits of life. It is necessary to be aware of the two varieties of physical evil because some efforts to solve the problem of physical evil may be adequate to one variety but not the other. Moreover, physical evil must not be viewed simply as an accidental even though frequent occurrence in the world. Physical evil seems to be involved in the very structure of the biological world. Individuals in every species, so to speak, depend for their very existence on the destruction of individuals in other species. The methods of slaughter, both in the animal and human realm, are fraught with suffering for the unlucky ones.

Moral evil, as we use it, denotes both moral wrong-doing such as lying, cheating, stealing, torturing, and murdering and character defects like greed, deceit, cruelty, wantonness, cowardice, and selfishness. These acts and traits may be judged either as intrinsically evil or as evil because they have painful consequences, but in either case the result is the same as far as the problem of evil is concerned. Moral evil, however construed, constitutes a double problem for one who believes in God. On the one hand, those who act wickedly debase their own character and, on the other, inflict terrible amounts of suffering on their fellow men.

II

The problem of evil has deeply affected many philosophers

and theologians, and they have responded to it in a number
of different ways. These responses sometimes seem bewildering
in their variety, and part of the point of this book is to introduce some order into this variety. Although there are variations
within types, there are, we believe, only four different ways
of responding to the problem of evil. The first strategy is to
evade the problem; the second is to show the problem to be
meaningless; the third is to try to solve the problem within a
traditional theistic framework; and the fourth is to modify
theistic concepts in the direction of a temporal and/or pantheistic
concept of God, and hence get rid of the problem of evil,
yet not go so far in this direction as to lose certain values
of theism. The first two types have in common the feature of
avoiding the problem in one way or another, while the latter
two have in common the feature of accepting the problem as
a legitimate one, one requiring an answer, and of making a
serious effort to solve it.

(A) The efforts to evade the problem are much alike,
although they arise from quite different backgrounds. Some
evasionists draw their inspiration from theologians like Karl
Barth and Paul Tillich, while others depend upon their interpretations of the later teachings of Wittgenstein. Indeed, some
evasionists depend upon both sources. Neo-orthodox theologians
evade the problem by saying that it is a part of rational theology,
and hence should be shunned at the outset. Commitment determines a "theological circle" which cannot be penetrated by
"foreign" criticisms like the problem of evil. The linguistic
philosophers claim that religious language is an autonomous
way of speaking, so that statements made within it are invulnerable to external criticisms. If one already *uses* religious
language he has no problem of evil. As we shall see, it is important to both the theologians and philosophers who employ
the present strategy to talk about "belief in" God rather than
"belief in the existence of" God.

(B) Recently a number of philosophers have attempted to
deny that there is a problem by showing that the problem
of evil is a meaningless one. The problem appears to have some
point at first glance, they say, but upon analysis turns out to

be a pseudo-difficulty, one arising from semantical misadventures. This move is a fascinating one because the same sort of strategy has been used for many years to deny cognitive content to any religious assertion whatever. The present strategy completely reverses the situation. It assumes the overall meaningfulness of religious assertions and then removes the most serious obstacle in the way of theistic belief by showing it to be based on semantical misconceptions. It must be clear, however, that these writers who would show the problem of evil to be meaningless do not depend upon a general theory of meaning in the way their adversaries do who declare all religious assertions meaningless. These writers base their claims of meaninglessness on alleged confusions indigenous to the problem of evil. The confusions allegedly found, as we shall see, differ radically in nature, but they all have the same goal, namely, eliminating the problem of evil as a pseudo-issue and thus removing the most persistent and formidable barrier in the path of theistic belief.

(C) Most religious writers reject evasion tactics as incompatible with theistic truth claims[7] and believe that the problem of evil is a meaningful one and hence requires a solution within the Christian framework. The point of such "solutions" is to show that evil is only *prima facie* gratuitous and not ultimately so. The solutions offered differ greatly in character. They may try to square evil with God's unlimited power and goodness where these latter concepts are interpreted quite strictly, or they may try to do it by "interpreting" or "loosening" these concepts without really abandoning them; e.g., a theist might argue that the experience of suffering and pain is necessary in order to produce spiritually significant human beings. The point is that the very concept of "being spiritually significant" *entails* the concept of "having suffered." Hence God is not limited in power because he cannot create spiritually significant beings at the outset. Or the theist might argue that God is all-good in some higher sense of "good" and hence does things that only appear to be evil from our fragmentary, ordinary moral perspectives. The sharp conflict that occasionally arises among theists reflects their disagreement about what basic strategy of reconciliation to pursue. The basic conflict is between those who do not want to stretch the concepts of unlimited power and goodness out of fear of losing them and those who want to stretch them out of fear of losing the reconciliation otherwise.

While the concepts of unlimited power and goodness figure most prominently in theistic discussions of evil there are other notions which play a crucial role upon occasion. These other notions are that God is separate from creation, exhibits attributes of personality, is Pure Form, determines and/or foresees all subsequent events, guarantees that good will eventually prevail over evil, and created the physical world *ex nihilo* (although versions of the Timaeus myth also occur).[8] It is important to be clear about all theistic assumptions because a number of them are rejected by those writers who depart from traditional views in the direction of temporalism and/or pantheism. It should be understood, of course, that theists do not always or even frequently agree upon the correct interpretation of these concepts and assumptions. Most recently, under the influence of philosophical language analysis, theists have attempted to avoid a straightforward descriptive interpretation and view them rather as models and metaphors designed to elicit and express a uniquely religious insight. The theodicies of all varieties of theism will be examined in detail in Chapters Four and Five. We shall range from St. Augustine, Descartes, Leibniz, and other giants of the theistic tradition to contemporary writers like Austin Farrer, John Hick, and Ian Ramsey who have managed to make theism much more acceptable to thoughtful people than was the case earlier in the century.

(D) The fourth strategy is to modify the metaphysical concepts of theism in the direction of a temporal and/or pantheistic concept of God. Many modern metaphysicians have tried this approach. The trouble with the theistic efforts to solve the problem of evil, they believe, is that they depend upon false metaphysics. They depend upon the traditional notions that God is unlimited in power, is outside of and not included in the universe, created the universe *ex nihilo*, is Pure Form and nontemporal in nature, and determined at the moment of creation the whole string of subsequent events. Deny one or more of these assumptions—depending upon the specific nature of your own system of metaphysics—and the problem of evil is solved, or disappears. If God is limited in power, evil occurs in spite of him; if God is not outside the universe, then evil is not something external to him to be eliminated but is a crucial part of God's own nature; and so on.

While these metaphysicians reject various theistic assumptions they are careful to retain others. They want to retain, among others, the notions that God is in some sense conscious, is a relevant object of worship, insures that good will eventually prevail, and is essentially compatible with the truths of the Judaeo-Christian religious (as distinct from theological) tradition. These metaphysicians, in short, are trying to combine a theistic concept of God, on the one hand, with temporal and pantheistic concepts, on the other. The quasi-theists, as we shall call them, suggest that with the proper metaphysics they can combine different conceptions of God in such a way that they retain the merits of all of them but avoid most of their faults. Of course, they wish to do this in order to deal with a host of theological riddles, but in dealing with the problem of evil in particular they wish to produce a conception of God that has all the worshipability of the traditional theistic God without the traits that create the problem of evil.

In modifying the traditional theistic conception of God it requires a new and elaborate metaphysics to make any progress in combining the desired traits of theism with those of temporalism and pantheism. Some of the most elaborate metaphysics produced for the sake of such a crossbreed (and for many other reasons) are those of Henri Bergson, H. N. Wieman, W. H. Sheldon, Louis Berman,, W. P. Montague, Joseph Le Conte, Samuel Alexander, Edgar Brightman, Alfred North Whitehead, Charles Hartshorne, and Josiah Royce. While they all make interesting metaphysical claims, they are not all equally successful in salvaging the crucial aspects of theism, namely, a personal God who is a relevant object of worship, one who insures that good will eventually prevail, and one who is compatible with the Judaeo-Christian tradition. Brightman,

Whitehead-Hartshorne, and Royce seem to be most successful in achieving the goal of quasi-theism and we shall accordingly treat them, in the proper place, in most detail.

Some comment on our four-way classification of responses to the problem of evil is necessary in order to forestall misunderstanding. First, it should be noticed that while there are four strategies, there are only two positions, namely, theism and quasi-theism (although, of course, there are many forms of the latter). The theist can either evade, deny, or solve the problem, while the quasi-theist, convinced of the significance of the problem and the impotence of theism in meeting it, can neither "deny" nor "solve" it. There is a sense, however, in which the quasi-theist, as well as the theist, can evade the problem. Tillich and Barth are examples of writers who qualify as both evasionists and quasi-theists. They qualify as the former because they refuse to allow the insolubility of the problem of evil as a good reason for not believing in God at all, but they both allow the difficulties over evil to modify the traditional theistic concept of God. For Tillich, e.g., God can no longer be understood as an all-powerful Being who ultimately turns all evil into good. Indeed, for him God cannot be understood as *a* Being at all but is rather "Being itself." Providence must be conceived as "God's directing creativity" working through the spontaneity of creatures and human freedom.[9] And sometimes Barth as a result of the problem of evil moves, in the words of John Hick, "half-way towards a Manichean dualism." On these occasions he argues that evil is *Das Nichtige,* which exists independently and thwarts God.[10]

Second, it must be understood that we are not suggesting that theism is still the official view of any particular historical religion, say Christianity, and that quasi-theism is "heretical." Never has Christian theology been less inclined toward heresy-hunting than it is today. Indeed, as we have just seen, Protestant neo-orthodoxy is often quasi-theistic in nature, while strands of Whitehead's metaphysics are everywhere present in Christian thought. And a substantial block of Protestant theology is still dominated by Brightman's concept of a finite god. In any case, it is sometimes difficult to tell the difference between certain types of theism and quasi-theism—to decide where the "stretching" of a theistic notion like omnipotence ends and where the quasi-theistic denial of it begins.

Finally, it must be understood that we do not use words such as *evasionist, traditional theist,* and *quasi-theist* with any intended negative connotations. We greatly respect all strategies employed and do not intend to denigrate any of them by our choice of names. "Evading income taxes" has a negative connotation, to be sure, but "evading a terrible danger" does not. And far from suggesting a disparagement of any view which it is used to qualify, *traditional* may well suggest a solid worth that should not be lightly disregarded. And *quasi-theism* is used in the straightforward descriptive sense of "partly theistic and partly not."

III

The thesis of this book is that neither theism nor quasi-theism is able to make sense of the facts of evil and that this incompetence constitutes a good reason for rejecting each one of them. The justification of this claim is threefold and will be developed in detail in the following chapters. First, we will show that it is necessary to take the problem of evil seriously, to play "for keeps" as the young player of marbles says. Evading and denying the problem will be shown to accomplish nothing. All efforts to evade the problem depend, in the long run, upon making religious beliefs immune to criticism. However, if there is no way in which it is appropriate or permissible to criticize a view, there is also no way in which it is appropriate or proper to adopt it. And it might be expected that all efforts to deny the problem would fail, since it seems too convenient that religious language in general should be meaningful while the main difficulty with religious cosmology should turn out to be a linguistic mistake.

Second, we show that the theistic effort to take the problem seriously fails. Each solution offered fails, in turn, to do the job required of it and no combination of them is sufficient to solve the various problems of physical and moral evil.[11] The crucial point, as we shall see, is that after a while objections begin to recur and to cluster in certain patterns. The inescapable conclusion arises that nothing new is being offered but only different permutations of solutions already shown to be deficient. The further the criticism of theodicies is pursued, the more confident one becomes that none will be successful in making sense of the facts of evil. (By "facts of evil" here we do not mean *prima facie* gratuitous evil but the "facts" as filtered through the dialectic of argument and counter-argument.) It is only fair to say, however, that the solutions offered vary a great deal in merit and that while some of them can be easily eliminated others are exceedingly subtle and sophisticated, both philosophically and theologically. Careful attention must be given to these latter arguments, and to our criticisms, because it is with them and their specified combinations that the theist either succeeds or fails in making his world view plausible.

Third, we show that the quasi-theistic effort to take the problem of evil seriously also fails. Each effort in turn fails to do the job required of it, partly for reasons indigenous to a particular view, partly for reasons indigenous to the *type* of quasi-theism involved, and partly for reasons that seem to apply generally to all views. An example of the latter is the difficulty quasi-theists have in escaping the anthropomorphic concept of a Being with personal attributes without falling into the opposite error of positing a Force, Principle, or Organic Whole which is religiously unavailable. It helps little to say that the Force, Principle, or Whole somehow also exhibits characteristics ordinarily ascribed to persons, since the question at issue is how this is possible.[12] Again, within types of quasi-theism, criticisms recur and cluster suggesting again that only permutations of a limited number of basic moves are being offered. The further such criticisms are pursued, the further *all* criticisms permeate one's consciousness and become absorbed into one's way of thinking, the more confident one becomes that no quasi-theism will both make sense of evil and convincingly maintain the personality of God, or both make sense of evil and convincingly maintain that good will prevail over evil in the long run.

There are several objections to the second and third claims above which need to be answered before these claims are substantiated in detail in later chapters.

(A) It might be objected that all we can hope to show is that no theodicy has yet successfully solved the problem or that no quasi-theism has yet successfully combined all the desirable characteristics into one concept of God, not that the problem is insoluble or that all quasi-theism is destined to fail. It is always logically possible that a new solution or a new quasi-theism will arise that will be successful. This objection, however, has little force. No one denies that success always remains a logical possibility for the religious cosmologist. The question is rather what likelihood is there, in view of the present state of evidence, that success will eventually occur? The answer is clearly that there is not only no evidence for the likelihood of such success but that the repeated failures, the recurrence and clustering of criticisms, the permutations of basic moves which have been found wanting, and the slight variations of old favorites count heavily against the likelihood of what no one denies is always a possibility.

Consider the case of a determined and ingenious tennis player who consistently loses key matches. He tries strategy after strategy and notices that with some strategies he loses less badly than with others. He is convinced that there is a strategy he has not yet tried which will lead to victory. Early in his career he expresses this conviction to friends and they are impressed by his determination. In year after year of his playing they marvel at this determination. After many years of experimenting with different strategies and consistently losing, he again expresses to friends his conviction that there must be an untried strategy that will bring victory. Although his friends still admire his energy and ingenuity, they now point out that it has become apparent that there are a limited number of strategies and in recent years he has merely repeated with only slight modification strategies used earlier; he continues to talk of finding a radically new strategy that will mean victory, but in fact he merely uses some permutation or combination of earlier strategies and calls it by a new name. While it is always logically possible that he may devise a new winning approach, in view of the available evidence such an outcome does not seem likely.

(B) It might also be objected that our conclusion does not follow from our premises. Even if the religious believer cannot make sense of the fact of evil, this failure does not constitute a good reason for not believing at all. This failure is genuinely embarrassing, to be sure, but is no cause for ultimate concern. The religious man has various grounds for believing in God—existential, historical, and rational—and thus knowing that God exists he knows that there is no genuine gratuitous evil in the world, that God has some purpose in all evil even though we do not know what it is.

This objection, however attractive it might seem at first glance, turns out to be ineffective. (i) It is essentially the "All's Well in God's View" version of the ultimate harmony solution to the problem of evil, and we shall discover numerous deficiencies with this view in Chapter Four. (ii) The logical and epistemological problems raised by historical grounds of belief are notorious and even more difficult to meet than the problem of evil. The existential grounds of belief, to be sure, are not to be dismissed lightly. However, there are existential grounds which pull the other way for those initially sensitive to the suffering of their fellows or those who become sensitive through discussions of the present problem. In fact, there is a terrible strain for many people because competing existential demands pull them mercilessly in opposite directions. (iii) Let us grant that any rational argument for the existence of God is valid. From premises *A* and *B* we infer correctly the conclusion *C* that God exists. But it does not follow that because *C* is correctly drawn there is no need to worry further about the believer's difficulties with the problem of evil. It is very easy to employ the same tactics in reverse. A naturalist might just as well say that the facts of evil convince him of the nonexistence of God and hence the falsity of *C*. Since *C* is validly inferred from *A* and *B* what the believer's argument really proves is the falsity of either *A* or *B*.

(iv) Even if historical, existential, or rational grounds for belief seemed convincing, there is nothing about any of them which would automatically override the grounds of disbelief produced by the problem of evil and other dysteleological aspects of the universe. Reasons for opposite conclusions would thus exist and such a situation no more justifies simple embarrassment for the believer than it does panic. There is a very real problem here about where the evidence points and the ground some people have for their agnosticism. (v) Finally, this maneuver has epistemic difficulties with the concept "to know."[13] Christians say they *know* that God exists in spite of the difficulty posed by the problem of evil (assuming, of course, for the moment, that the problem *is* insurmountable). However, in order to say that he *knows* that God exists, the Christian must not simply be certain of being right and happen in fact to be right, but he must have evidence adequate to warrant his degree of confidence. And he does not have adequate evidence to warrant his confidence when he ignores such negative evidence as that presented by the riddle of God and evil. Unless such major difficulties as this one are removed, the Christian cannot legitimately take the existence of God as known. It may well be, again, that any argument in favor of believing should be interpreted as a disproof of one or more of its premises.

Before beginning our detailed analyses it is necessary to be quite clear about the *extent* of our claims in order to avoid misunderstanding. We are claiming that neither theism nor quasi-theism is able both to make sense of the facts of evil and to have an acceptable concept of God, and that this incompetence constitutes a good reason for rejecting each one of them. We add at this time that this incompetence (if we do show it to be an incompetence) seems to constitute a good reason for rejecting any religious cosmology whatever. It might seem premature to go directly from a rejection of theism and quasi-theism to a rejection of all religious cosmology, since clearly we have not considered all possible views about the nature of God. We nowhere consider the possibility of a purely pantheistic God or a God unlimited in power and evilness. We do, however, have reasons for these omissions and believe that they justify proceeding directly from a rejection of theism and quasi-theism to a rejection of religious cosmology altogether. The pantheistic concept of God, to be sure, avoids the problem of evil, but such a concept, referring as it does to a "being" indistinct from creation, impersonal, no object of worship, and no guarantor of the triumph of good, appears to be, except for the odd metaphysics upon which it is built, indistinguishable from the naturalism which we accept. The greatness of a quasi-theist like Royce is to realize this point at the same time he realizes the inability of theism to cope with the problem of evil and to try to avoid both faults in a new "hybrid" concept. Moreover, we do not ignore the possibility of an all-powerful, all-evil God because we think it is a silly notion—far from it—but because it would encounter a corresponding problem of good which would be isomorphic in reverse with the problem of evil and equally devastating in its implications. (This notion of a problem of the good we will develop in detail in our discussion of evasion tactics.)

The extent of our claim, however, must be clarified further. While we are claiming that the facts of evil constitute a good reason for rejecting all religious cosmology, we are *not* claiming that they constitute a sufficient reason for such rejection. The problem of evil is one part of a complex of problems all components of which must be considered before any reasonable final decision can be reached. There are historical, existential, and rational grounds which have been offered as good reasons for *accepting* a religious outlook, and one has to analyze and criticize them effectively and in detail before claiming that the facts of evil constitute a sufficient reason for rejecting religion. We do, of course, believe that these alleged grounds can be rebutted and that the facts of evil thus constitute a sufficient reason for rejecting religious belief, but we do not attempt such a rebuttal here. We are solely concerned with showing that difficulties with evil constitute a good reason for rejecting religious belief.

In mounting a full scale philosophical alternative there would be a number of further problems requiring careful scrutiny. It would be necessary to show, e.g., that the *prima facie* teleological aspects of the world can be explained naturalistically and that the place of value in such a world is neither minimized nor ignored. (Indeed, the naturalist will stress the absolute importance of moral endeavor in the world as he conceives it. There is no longer any guaranteed outcome. Dedicated moral effort must lie behind whatever justice there is in the world.) Again, while we do believe that these issues can be met satisfactorily we shall not deal with them in this book. The riddle of God and evil is sufficiently difficult to keep us occupied for a good while. It is certainly a key issue in the complex question of religious belief. There are writers on both sides of the issue, in fact, who believe it to be *the* key issue.

NOTES

1. This point applies to George Schlesinger's "The Problem of Evil and the Problem of Suffering," *American Philosophical Quarterly*, I:244-47, 1964.
2. The problem of evil is frequently formulated in this way. Cf. Nelson Pike, "God and Evil: A Reconsideration," *Ethics*, LXVIII:119, 1958; Nelson Pike, "Hume on Evil," *Philosophical Review*, LXXII, reprinted in Pike (Ed.), *God and Evil*, Englewood Cliffs, Prentice-Hall, 1964, pp. 85-102; and Terence Penelhum, "Divine Goodness and the Problem of Evil," *Religious Studies*, II:95-107, 1966.
3. Mark Pontifex: "The Question of Evil," in *Prospect for Metaphysics*, edited by Ian Ramsey, London, George Allen and Unwin Ltd., 1961, p. 137; and Alvin Plantinga, "The Free-Will Defence," in *Philosophy In America*, edited by Max Black, London, George Allen and Unwin Ltd., 1965, pp. 219-220.
4. Penulhum, *op. cit.*, p. 103.
5. Pike, "God and Evil: A Reconsideration," pp. 118-19.
6. See John Hick's *Philosophy of Religion*, Englewood Cliffs, Prentice-Hall, 1963, p. 41.
7. See John Hick's "Sceptics and Believers," in *Faith and the Philosophers*, edited by John Hick, New York, St. Martin's Press, 1964, pp. 235-50.
8. Many of these tenets are, of course, as old as Christianity even though the term "theism" is an invention of the 17th century. Cf. V. Ferm, (Ed.), *An Encyclopedia of Religion*, Paterson, Littlefield, Adams, 1959.
9. Paul Tillich: *Systematic Theology*. Chicago, University of Chicago Press, 1963, Vol. III, p. 372.
10. For a criticism of such a solution see John Hick, *Evil and the God of Love*, New York, Harper and Row, 1966, pp. 143-50 and p. 193. It is clear that Barth's theory of *Das Nichtige* cannot even satisfy the more careful believers much less satisfy those who have doubts.

11. See J. L. Mackie's review of John Hick's *Evil and the God of Love* in *Philosophical Books, III*:17, 1966. "In a wide-ranging historical survey, and in his own struggle to develop a solution, Hick provides an unintentional confirmation of the claim I made in an article in *Mind* eleven years ago: All the possible solutions of the problem of evil can be grouped under a small number of headings and then can be systematically shown to be inadequate as defences of orthodox theism." Cf. Mackie's "Evil and Omnipotence," *Mind, LXIV*, 1955, reprinted in Pike's *God and Evil*, pp. 46-60.

12. It is not helpful either to refer to God as "the something personal in things at large, not itself a person," as Virgil Aldrich does in his "Tinkling Symbols," in *Faith and the Philosophers*, edited by John Hick, p. 53. Also pp. 49-53. Ian T. Ramsey is no more successful in his effort to get the "personal" and "impersonal" models and metaphors of God talk into one "super-model." See Chapter III of his *Christian Discourse*, London, Oxford U.P., 1965.

13. See Antony Flew's *God and Philosophy*, London, Hutchinson and Co., 1966, p. 59.

Chapter Two

On the Difficulty of Evading the Problem

I

THERE HAVE BEEN many attempts to make religious belief, commitment, and language immune to criticism and to make ordinary and scientific concepts of evidence irrelevant to them. The point of such attempts is to evade the usual critiques of historical religion, the problems posed by higher criticism, conflicts with science, and epistemic discussions about adequate evidence. To some religious people this tactic has seemed to have an application to the problem of evil, although others have felt that while the position in general is right it has no application to the problem of evil. Our contention is that the position not only has no application to the problem of evil but is implausible in general; hence that not only is the difficulty with evil a good reason for rejecting religion but that the traditional critiques, for anything this position shows to the contrary, also constitute good reasons for such rejection.

The general evasionist view is established or justified by radically different means even though the final result is identical. Recent attempts to establish the view reflect the influence of Karl Barth and Paul Tillich, on the one hand, and certain interpretations of the later Wittgenstein and J. L. Austin, on the other. We will briefly explain each justification in turn and then show why none of them either has an application to the problem of evil or is tenable in its own right.

(A) According to Barth, the whole of rational theology is not only useless but exhibits on the part of those who indulge in it a sinful nature.[1] It is useless because rational arguments are irrelevant to the true basis of belief and pernicious because

20

it recognizes by implication the legitimacy of the traditional rational critiques of historical Christianity. [Rational theology in all aspects is sinful because it puts human reason above revelation. It is the sin of intellectual pride, the old sin of seeking to eat of the tree of the knowledge of good and evil.[2] Barth's advice is to abandon such theology and return to Reformation concepts. Man has a completely corrupt nature and can have no insight into religious truth through any human capacity whatever. Belief and salvation come to some wholly through the grace of God. *Fides sola gratia* is the watchwood of neo-orthodoxy. Moreover, although revelation is granted to some people, they can never know that they have been the recipients of it. Man, in short, has no point of contact with the divine. The only thing he can do is hope and worship.[3]

While Barth rejects natural theology he is not simply an irrationalist. He does not wholly eschew "reason" but rather locates and interprets it in his own special way. Reason, he thinks, consists in conforming to the *object* of knowledge, not in ratiocination, and in the case of religion this means conforming to the content of *revelation*.[4] The Christian Revelation, in turn, he tries to show is *the* Revelation. It is in this sense that Barth is said by some "to adjust assent to the evidence." Such evidence, he seems to think, is conclusive. If a theologian accepts the Christian Revelation and exhibits believing obedience, he becomes invulnerable to external criticism. "If revelation of this kind is reflected upon by those who claim it and the result is called theology, where is there access for the nontheological critic? The method and structure of theology thus conceived can be criticized only in intra-theological debate, which is what Barth intends."[5]

(B) Tillich rejects natural theology on existential grounds. "In every assumedly scientific theology," he writes, "there is a point where individual experience, traditional valuation, and personal commitment must decide the issue."[6] However metaphysical or empirical one's concept of God may be, it is really based on an immediate experience of ultimate value and being of which one can become intuitively aware.[7] All rational justifications for believing in God only confirm what was present from the beginning. Conversely, no rational arguments against such a belief are effective because, coming from another frame of reference, they are "foreign," "external," "outside," and hence irrelevant. This is what Tillich calls "the theological circle."

Tillich is eager to show that Christianity, while basically existential and voluntaristic, is not irrational in the sense of being self-contradictory or demanding assent to the absurd.[8] Consider the doctrine of the logos made flesh in Jesus the Christ. This claim that Christ unites universal Being in concrete form is not a genuinely self-contradictory claim. It is not like saying that this table is black and white all over at the same moment. It is rather a *paradoxical* claim that adumbrates a dynamic, Hegelian-like ontology that is at odds only with Aristotle's static ontology, not with his law of noncontradiction. While such a paradoxical claim is not self-contradictory, it is, Tillich contends, not a matter of rational apprehension either. Ultimately, all Christian paradoxes transcend reason. "This is indicated by the ecstatic state in which all biblical and classical theological *paradoxa* appear."[9] Paradoxes, in short, are simply fumbling cognitive ways of pointing toward spiritual truths that can never be adequately pictured.

(C) The existential theological circle has been transformed by some writers into a linguistic theological circle.[10] Intelligibility takes many and varied forms, the argument goes, but there is no norm for intelligibility "in general." Criteria of logic arise in the contexts of "ways of living" or "modes of social life" and only make sense in their respective frameworks. Science, for example, is one such mode of life and religion is another, and each has criteria of intelligibility peculiar to itself. "So within science or religion actions can be logical or illogical; in science, for example, it would be illogical to refuse to be bound by the results of a properly carried out experiment; in religion it would be illogical to suppose that one could pit one's own strength against God's; and so on. But we cannot sensibly say that either the practice of science itself or that of religion is either illogical or logical; both are nonlogical."[11] The specific frameworks themselves provide the criteria for some special kind of sense and logic. The implication of all this is that any frame of reference, any way of living or mode of social life, provides its own autonomous and unassailable language system. Given the fact that the language-game of religion is played there simply is no way in which it can be logically inappropriate or improper to engage in it. It simply cannot be criticized from the outside; indeed, it cannot even be *understood* from the outside.

Those who use different variants of the linguistic circle maneuver agree on the importance of distinguishing between "belief in" God and "belief in the existence of" God, and at this point are all agreeing with their neo-orthodox and existentialist conterparts.[12] "Belief in" God is a genuinely religious concept while "belief in the existence of" God is a scientific type notion to which rational, nonreligious criteria of evidence are applicable. To ask the question in a religious context is to mix modes of life inadmissibly and to invite confusion. The religious man does not talk *about* God but talks *to* him. When someone says "I believe in God the father Almighty" he is not asserting that he believes that God exists but is *performing an act* through the use of these words which makes perfectly good sense and is unassailable within its own frame of reference.

Our reply to these evasions, as we indicated, is twofold. We will attempt to show that none of them has an application to the problem of evil and that all are implausible in general and hence no detriment to the many traditional criticisms of religion they were designed to meet.

(i) The problem of evil, it must be noted at once, is neither a part of rational theology nor a criticism that is imposed upon religious belief from some external frame of reference. Thus all the present evasion efforts are simply irrelevant to the problem of evil. To classify the discussion of God and evil as rational theology is to confuse the two notions of rational theology and being rational about theology. The former requires reasons for believing in God, while the latter requires only that beliefs about God, on whatever grounds they are held, cohere and match in some intelligible way. This does not mean that there is no room in religion for paradoxes and mysteries like "the logos made flesh," but it does mean that there is no room for absurdity and incompatibility. Neo-orthodox writers certainly agree to this stipulation. Now the point is that there is *prima facie* gratuitous evil in the world which never gets resolved by the recurring combinations of old solutions, a deficiency which suggests that there is a real incompatibility or nonmatching of beliefs in a theistic framework. This nonmatching of beliefs is not a paradox or mystery in the supposedly admissible sense but is an absurdity or incompatibility of the type neo-orthodox writers in other contexts renounce. Moreover, to be puzzled by this difficulty and seek an answer (or even to be persuaded that it has no solution and thus counts as a good reason for rejecting religious belief) is certainly not to exhibit sinful pride. The effort to make one's views a coherent whole is not a matter of sitting in judgment upon God but is rather an effort to *understand* what it is one believes. Such "reasonableness" can be viewed by a godly man as just as much a divine gift as faith and consequently no more vain than the latter. Indeed, some Christian writers think that the charge of pride and vanity might well be made of neo-orthodoxy rather than of those thinkers who try to solve the problem.[13]

Finally, the problem of *prima facie* gratuitous evil is clearly not a problem forced upon theism from an external frame of reference that has different concepts of evidence and reasonableness. It is a problem wholly indigenous to the religious frame of reference and requires a reexamination of basic concepts within that system. The problem is either how to stretch the three concepts of evil and God's unlimited power and goodness without actually abandoning one or more of them as quasi-theists do, or how to match up the three concepts if they are interpreted in a strict and traditional way. In either case, the problem is completely internal and a matter of being reasonable about theology and not a matter of imposing foreign concepts of evidence upon theology.

(ii) Barth's notion that reason consists in conforming to the nature of an object and not being misled by rational artifacts and that this conformity is only legitimately achieved through the Christian Revelation is itself a staggering epistemological claim that would require enormous skill to justify. Barth clearly does not display such skill in his earlier "Kantian" and later "Hegelian-like" philosophical speculations. But the important point for us is that getting involved in philosophical justifications of what counts as being "reasonable" itself detracts in a damaging fashion from the dramatic and appealing claim that philosophy is irrelevant to theological claims and that religious commitment and revelation constitute an unchallengeable frame of reference. It is this claim that has seemed most important to those neo-orthodox writers who wish to evade the problem of evil.

(iii) Tillich says that the theological circle is existentially grounded. The argument from existential commitment, however, is a double-edged sword and cuts both ways. A feeling for the depth and pervasiveness of evil is so great in some people that Christianity is not even a live hypothesis for them. They can stand gratuitous evil if it comes from a naturalistic world that knows neither good nor bad or comes from a genuinely evil world, but they could not bear to hear from any providential source whatever that it is not really gratuitous evil after all—that there is some point to it. Tillich sometimes seems to be aware of this existential dimension of the problem of evil, but he does not, after all, understand it.[14] The existential feel for evil, he says, must be taken into account in any adequate conception of divine providence. It rules out optimistic theodicies, progressive theology, and so on. But this response quite misses the point. For some people the existential — feel for evil constitutes the grounds for not believing in God at all, or for others like Schopenhauer constitutes the grounds for believing that an evil will dominates reality. In either case the existential feel for evil does not simply set the requirement of pessimism which any acceptable theodicy must meet. It is a bit too convenient for Tillich to use existential grounds as the basis of a theological circle and then use counter existential grounds to provide a particular kind of theodicy!

(iv) The distinction between "belief in" and "belief that" is an important one, to be sure, but both existential and linguistic proponents of "the circle" are misled by it. To say that "I believe in God the father Almighty . . . ," as in the

Apostle's and Nicene Creed, *is* to perform an act and not to assert a proposition just as the minister who says "I baptize you in the name of Jesus Christ" is performing an act and not asserting a proposition. Yet while performative utterances are neither true nor false, are not themselves statements, nevertheless they usually entail assertions which are either true or false.[15] Saying the Apostle's Creed is an act of faith, adoration, and commitment without doubt, but it entails the claim that God is almighty and infinitely good. But such claims do not match up with the admitted instances of *prima facie* gratuitous evil. Then the stretching of concepts begins. If one stretches the concepts too far or abandons one or more of them, then it becomes pointless for such a person to continue the use of performative utterances like the Nicene Creed. The same can be said, we claim, for every set of performatives that has been put in place of the rejected one. None of them is any more effective in dealing with the problem of evil and hence every alternate set of performatives is equally pointless to pursue. The crucial point is that we are not importing cognitive considerations about "the existence of God" into a framework of "belief in" God. These two notions should be kept distinct. What we have shown is that questions of truth and falsity arise within a theological context and that the inability to match these truth claims causes internal questions about the nature and existence of God. Questions about "the existence of God" are not present at the beginning; they arise, rather, as a result of taking the religious circle quite seriously. Is this not the route travelled by most thoughtful and noncompulsive agnostics, humanists, and naturalists?

(v) The very concept of a theological circle encounters serious difficulty. If the claims implicit in it were true, it would make the use of any particular frame of reference wholly arbitrary. But certainly it is possible to discuss the consistency, adequacy, and genuineness of different frames and hence arrive at good reasons for accepting some, and rejecting those incompatible with the ones accepted. It is true that all systematic arguments and justifications of particular judgments must occur within a frame of reference, but it is also true that good reasons (including reference to existential and historical matters as well as "rational" considerations) can be given why one framework should be adopted or rejected. One is inconsistent, inadequate, and so on. Or one is apparently consistent, adequate, genuine, and so on. As involved and subtle as this sort of indirect argument is, to deny the possibility of it is to land in skepticism, not Christianity. If there is no way in which it is permissible or appropriate to criticize or evaluate a frame of reference, then there appears to be no way in which it is appropriate or proper to engage in it. One simply engages in it, and there is an end of the matter. But the same could be said for *any* frame of reference and hence the notion of the applicability of any frame to our particular world is forfeited. But this conclusion certainly must be unacceptable to the Christian who clearly believes that his performative frame of reference entails claims that are true while all others entail at least some that are false.

The present point may be put another way that may help the "light dawn" or "the penny drop." The concept of a theological circle produces the following alternatives: either one can insist that the Christian commitment is the right one simply because one feels it to be so, or one can give some reason for accepting it. The first alternative is useless since everyone, including those who have opposite commitments, feels that his "belief in" is the right one. The second alternative is more promising. One can justify his Christian commitment by pointing out both internal and external evidences of divine revelation, by showing how it is morally superior to other religions, by successfully rebutting criticisms of the commitment, and so on. But these reasons for justifying the Christian frame of reference are themselves arguable and hence the notion of a theological circle which is immune to examination has disappeared. The same point can be made again in the context of apologetic theology. Tillich claims that the task of apologetic theology is to "show that trends which are immanent in all religions and culture move toward the Christian answer."[16] But this claim forcibly rejects the notion of all other autonomous frames of reference and hence entails, *even if the claim were a true one,* that Christianity itself does not constitute a frame of reference immune to criticism.

(vi) The previous criticisms apply in large measure to the notion of a linguistic as well as a theological circle. There are, however, in addition, difficulties which are unique to the former. In the first place the criteria of intelligibility and rationality implicit in the practice of a society or of a mode of social life are often incoherent and often do not yield one clear and unambiguous answer. "When this is the case people start questioning their own criteria. They try to criticize the standards of intelligibility and rationality which they have held hitherto."[17] On the view that a given linguistic circle *defines* such standards it is difficult to make sense of such criticisms. Yet the criticism is clearly legitimate. Hence doubts arise about the concept of a linguistic circle. In the second place, the dichotomy between some overall criterion of intelligibility "in general" and the complete relativism of criteria determined by discrete linguistic circles is a false one. Criteria themselves have a history. They change, grow, and develop and hence are not simply defined by a given frame of reference. The propositions of Azande witchcraft, e.g., are *in principle* falsifiable but are *in fact* unfalsifiable. There are ways of covering all negative cases. Now how can such a frame of reference be criticized and by what standards? "It seems . . . that one could only hold the belief of the Azande rationally *in the absence of* any practice of science and technology in which criteria of effectiveness, ineffectiveness and kindred notions had been built up. But to say this is to recognize the appropriateness of scientific criteria of judgment from our standpoint. The Azande do not intend their belief either as a piece of science or as a piece of non-science. They do not possess these categories. It is only *post eventum*, in the light of later and more sophisticated understanding that their beliefs and concepts can be classified and evaluated at all."[18]

II

Tillich's thought is relevant to the problem of evil in more ways than we have yet discussed. His own rational theodicy is carefully thought out and rewards close attention.

For a believer, Tillich says, the existence of *prima facie* gratuitous evil does not constitute a reason for giving up his belief in God but simply constitutes one of the ultimate mysteries of religion.[19] And yet, he feels, within the religious framework there is not only the possibility of a rational theodicy but also a grave need for it. While *prima facie* gratuitous evil never constitutes a reason for giving up a belief in God, such evil cannot be ignored. It sets certain rational requirements for Christian theology.[20] It eliminates the theological optimism which characterized Enlightenment theodicies and the progressivism which characterized nineteenth and early twentieth century theology. And it requires certain modifications of the traditional Christian conceptions of God and divine providence. God can no longer be understood as an all-powerful Being who ultimately turns all evil into good. (In fact, he cannot be understood as *a* Being at all but the Ground of Being.) No future justice and happiness can annihilate or justify the suffering and injustice of the past. And providence can no longer be understood in a deterministic way—as if God had built in a design at creation and occasionally intervenes miraculously when necessary. Providence rather must be conceived as "God's directing creativity" working through the spontaneity of creatures and human freedom.[21] Man is born with the "freedom for good and evil," and his decisions and acts are effectual in bringing about a different future than would have occured without them.

The crucial question, of course, is how "God's directing creativity" works through the spontaneity of creatures and human freedom. At this point Tillich returns from his rational journey. The way in which it works "is identical with the divine mystery and beyond calculation and description."[22] Hegel made the mistake of trying to describe how it works by applying the dialectics of logic to the concrete events of history. His mistake was trying to understand how providence works overall. It was a grandiose attempt to "set himself on the chair of the divine providence." Fragmentary insights into the workings of providence are possible but that is all; the whole understanding "remains hidden in the mystery of the divine life."[23]

Tillich's notion of mystery and his rational theodicy are

skillfully enough developed but something seems to be wrong with each at the outset.

(A) The notion of mystery as used by Tillich is dubious in several ways. First, he provides no criterion for delimiting the area of mystery in such a way that not all parties in a fundamental dispute can invoke it. Everyone can protect his own commitment by invoking some notion of mystery and no one thereby gets any closer to resolving whatever question is at issue. And even if he were to provide such a criterion, it is difficult to see how he could apply it consistently, or in a nonquestion-begging way.

Second, and equally fundamental, Tillich's notion of mystery does not really evade the problem of evil. What, after all, does it mean to say that evil constitutes one of the ultimate mysteries of religion? It might mean that evil serves some purpose but it is a mystery what it is. Or it might mean that it is a mystery whether or not evil serves some purpose. In the first case, there must be independent existential, historical, and rational grounds for claiming that God exists and that evil thus serves some purpose though we do not know what it is. We have, however, shown in detail what is wrong with this view in Chapter One. On the other hand, if what is meant is that it is a mystery whether or not evil serves some ends, then no evasion, solution, or anything whatever to ease the problem of evil has been offered.

(B) The rational part of Tillich's theodicy exhibits the same deficiencies found in other quasi-theistic theodicies. Tillich is right in believing that the traditional Christian view of God's all-powerfulness and the mechanical notion of providence must be abandoned in view of the existence of monstrous moral and physical evil. However, Tillich's alternative encounters equal difficulty. In the first place it is unclear how Tillich's God is religiously available. It seems strange to pray to "the Ground of Being." And it is unclear how any personal attributes are applicable to it. Moreover, it is difficult to see how, on Tillich's view, "the ultimate triumph of God's aims" is assured. The strength of the traditional view is that an all-powerful God can assure such a triumph. On Tillich's view, however, God must work through man's freedom and other restrictions in order to achieve his goals. But it is a little too convenient to deny the unlimited power of God in order to account for evil and yet allow him precisely that amount of power which insures the ultimate triumph of God's aims. And, finally, Tillich never succeeds in making it clear how God's directing creativity and man's freedom are ultimately compatible.

(C) Tillich's tumbling act—going from a notion of mystery, to rational theodicy, and back to mystery—is not without difficulties. He appears to want to play the game of theodicy and yet not. One can have a rational theodicy but never one that can be destroyed by counterreasons. The notion of mystery is always in the background. Such rules hardly seem fair. It is like playing chess in the following strange way. By virtue of playing you accept the rules that the queen starts on its own color, has the equivalent mobility of a rook and a bishop, and so on. But when you are checkmated you want to avoid disaster by saying that a king, after all, in some mysterious cases, can move two places. You avoid defeat finally by sweeping the players off the board and into the box. You did not lose, to be sure, but then you really did not play the game either.

(D) Tillich's notions of paradox and symbolism suggest a final avenue of evasion which must be sealed off if our analysis is to be complete. Tillich assures us that Christian paradoxes are not self-contradictory. They point to spiritual truths which cannot be expressed in terms of "the structure of reason" but only in terms of "the depth of reason."[24] Jesus the Christ is the concrete Absolute—this is the most fundamental Christian paradox. Yet if one tries to pinpoint the concrete nature of Christ or the absolute nature of the logos, the paradoxical truth of their union disappears. "The words of Jesus and the apostles point to this New Being; they make it visible through stories, legends, symbols, paradoxical descriptions, and theological interpretations. But none of these expressions of the experience of the final revelation is final and absolute in itself. They are all conditioned, relative, open to change and additions."[25] This viewpoint, it should be clear, permits systematic evasion. Whatever criticism is levelled against Christianity Tillich can allow.

"We have constantly to get rid of false conceptions of God." It allows Tillich to be critical of *any* actual form of Christianity and still be committed to Christianity; it allows him to admit deficiencies in every concrete formulation of Christianity and yet say that the Christian way is the true way—a paradox which passes understanding literally. Either Christianity says something or it does not, and it is vulnerable either way. Tillich's strategy at this point seems highly dubious. It amounts to having a blank check which is never written on or writing a promissory note that can never be called in. To write "Love" finally on the blank check neither shows any significant insight into what is unique in Christ's message nor is itself immune to criticism.[26]

III

There are, as we have seen, numerous ways of trying to evade the problem of evil. We have examined them in detail, both in the present and previous chapter, and have rejected them with what we take to be good reasons. There is, however, a final indirect sort of criticism which we want to offer as a critique of all types of evasion. It is formulated in the context of mysticism but could be adapted to any variety of the evasion strategy. That it is a whimsical argument will become evident by and by, but this quality, we hope, will not obscure the dead earnestness and significant points it contains.

The usual naturalistic way of explaining mystical experiences is well known. They are explained away by the concepts of abnormal psychology; they are results, some say, of hallucination, delusion, hypnosis, paranoia, etc. Indeed, if Saint Joan were alive today, hearing voices as she did, she would be committed immediately to a state mental hospital. However, we find it difficult to look at Saint Joan, Saint Theresa, and Saint John of the Cross in this way. Rather we shall accept all Christian mystical experiences at face value—assuming that they have significant religious meaning for those who experience them. Christian mysticism, however, is not the only kind. We have a friend who reported having a mystical experience with an all-powerful, all-evil God—"It was ghastly," he said, shaking even at the recollection of it. (If you do not choose to believe this, no matter; just consider that it is still a logical possibility.)

What now can the theists say to our friend? How can they show him to be wrong, for his sake and for their own peace of mind? They might, of course, explain the experience away by various hypotheses: he was drunk, he has a persecution complex, or whatever. But this tactic will not do; we have agreed that we would not explain away the Christian mystic's experience in such ways, but would accept it at face value. So, too, must the Christian accept our friend's experience at face value.

The theists, of course, still want mightily to show that our friend is mistaken. What can they say by way of rational argument to show that he is wrong? Why, they can point out to him that he has an insoluble problem of good on his hands. If God is all-powerful and all-evil, how can you explain the enormous amount of apparently unnecessary physical and moral good in the world? Consider, e.g., how the soil, rain, and sunshine produce our crops and how many men have sacrificed themselves for the good of others. Our friend sees that he has a problem but replies in the following way: Yes, but I can square God's character with good by a contrast theory. Good is necessary as a contrast so that we shall be able properly to understand and feel the horror of evil. The theist objects that we do not need so much good to achieve this goal. Our friend agrees, but offers another theory: It is man's free will, he says, which solves his problem. God granted man free will, knowing full well how he would use it to produce some good. Unhappily, of course, if he is to have free will, he must be capable of doing good also. The theist objects that God's omniscience and man's free will are incompatible concepts. Our friend is forced to agree, but offers another theory: It is, he says, the ultimate disharmony theory. What human beings call good is an event seen out of context, in isolation, and since man has only a fragmentary view of events, this is the only way he can see it. God, however, who has an overall view of events, sees how such events are evil in the long run or evil from an overall viewpoint. The theist objects that if one is not competent to know how good leads to evil, then he is not competent to judge evil either; for all he knows it might lead to good eventually. Our friend retreats before this argument, but he has another— however, it is not necessary to go further! The point should be perfectly clear by now that the problems of evil and good are completely isomorphic; what can be said about the one can be said about the other in reverse. For any solution to one problem there is a parallel solution to the other, and for every counter-argument in the one there is a parallel counter-argument in the other.

There are two conclusions, or morals, to be drawn from our whimsical discussion of the problem of good.

(A) *All we ask the theist is to let others do unto him as he would do unto them.* If people hold a position opposed to him and buttressed on the same ground of mysticism, or any other nonrational ground, he would wish to dissuade them from their view by rational argument in spite of their basing it on such experience. We simply wish to do the same to the theist. We do not say that he should ignore existential matters and rely on argument alone, but we do suggest that he temper his mystical thought, or whatever else it may be, with a good dose of thought about his problem of evil, and check finally to see which way it goes.

(B) It is an interesting and ironic consequence of the problem of good that the theist cannot have what he wants both ways. He would like the problem of evil to be soluble, since he would dispose of the strongest antitheistic argument thereby. On the other hand, he would like the problem of good to be insoluble, because this insolubility would be the best reason possible for giving up belief in an all-powerful, all-evil god. (By the way, the notion of an evil god is not all whimsy. It is difficult indeed to dispose of such a concept.) Unfortunately for the theist, he cannot have it both ways. Since the two problems are entirely isomorphic, if one is soluble so is the other, and if one is insoluble so is the other. The theist must choose one way or the other and lose something important either way he chooses.

NOTES

1. Karl Barth: *The Epistle to the Romans*, 6th ed., translated by Edwyn C. Hoskyns, London, Oxford U. P., 1933; *Dogmatics in Outline*, translated by G. T. Thomson, New York, Philosophical Library, N. D.; *Church Dogmatics*, vol. 1, translated by G. T. Thomson, Edinburgh, T. G. T. Clark, 1936.

2. In this connection Barth speaks of "temptation," "illegitimate desire," and "unhealthy pride." *Church Dogmatics*, vol. I, p. 186.

3. In *God Here and Now*, New York, Harper and Row, 1964, p. 31, Barth writes that "because it is free grace, the proclamation of the Church cannot deal with any characteristics, capacities, points of contact, and the like which might be credited on the human side, or with any human potentialities or merits which should be taken into consideration. It is grace for creatures to whom God owes nothing, nothing at all."

4. Barth, *Church Dogmatics*, vol. 1, pp. 214, 280. Cf. *Faith and the Philosophers*, edited by John Hick, New York, St. Martin's Press, 1964, pp. 159-222.

5. Edward A. Dowey: "But is it Barth?" In Hick's *Faith and the Philosophers*, pp. 204-05.

6. Paul Tillich: *Systematic Theology*. Chicago, University of Chicago Press, 1951, vol. I, p. 8.

7. *Ibid.*, p. 9.

8. *Ibid.*, pp. 56-57, Cf. pp. 16-18, 150-53.

9. *Ibid.*, p. 57.

10. See Peter Winch, *The Idea of a Social Science and its Relation to Philosophy*, London, Routledge and Kegan Paul, 1958. Cf. Alasdair MacIntyre's "Is Understanding Religion Compatible with Believing?" in Hick's *Faith and the Philosophers*, pp. 119-124.

11. Winch, *op. cit.*, pp. 100-101; quoted by MacIntyre.

12. See Norman Malcolm's "Is It a Religious Belief that 'God Exists'?" in Hick's *Faith and the Philosophers*, pp. 103-110, and his "Anselm's Ontological Arguments," *Philosophical Review*, LXIX:41-62, 1960. Cf. John Hick's "Sceptics and Believers" in *Faith and the Philosophers*, pp. 235-242, and Antony Flew's *God and Philosophy*, London, Hutchinson and Co., 1966, pp. 173-77. Also Flew, pp. 79, 81.

13. H. J. Paton: *The Modern Predicament*. New York, Collier Books, 1962, p. 52.

14. Tillich, *Systematic Theology*, vol. III, p. 372.

15. J. L. Austin: *Philosophical Papers*. London, Oxford U.P., 1961, p. 224.

16. Tillich, *Systematic Theology*, vol. I, p. 15.

17. Alasdair MacIntyre, *op. cit*, pp. 121-22.

18. *Ibid.*, p. 121.

19. Tillich, *Systematic Theology*, vol. III, pp. 372-74.
20. *Ibid.*, pp. 372-73. Tillich's quasi-theism has appealed to many of the now widely discussed "Death of God" theologians. Much of John A. T. Robinson's *Honest to God*, Philadelphia, The Westminster Press, 1963, is an exposition of Tillich; *Radical Theology and the Death of God* by Thomas J. J. Altizer and William Hamilton, Indianapolis, Bobbs-Merrill, 1966, is dedicated to Tillich. They are drawn to Tillich's famous polemic against theism (i.e. against belief in God as *a* being). Many of these theologians use Tillich's metaphysics of "the ground of being" to develop what is supposed to be a nontheistic version of Christianity. Of course, insofar as the "Death of God" theologians are simply humanists with the addition of a little traditional religious language we have no quarrel with them. It is only when they attempt to reintroduce by means of a novel metaphysics many of the elements of a traditional theism in what amounts to a quasi-theism (as the figures we discuss in Chapter Six do) that we object. For a criticism of Tillich's own attempt to do this see Peter H. Hare, "Religion and Analytic Naturalism," *Pacific Philosophy Forum*, V:52-61, 1967.
21. Tillich, *Systematic Theology*, vol. III, p. 372.
22. *Ibid.*, p. 373.
23. *Ibid.*, p. 374.
24. *Ibid.*, vol. I, p. 150.
25. *Ibid.*, vol. 1, p. 151. Cf. Tillich's "The Meaning and Justification of Religious Symbols" in S. Hook, (Ed.), *Religious Experience and Truth*, New York, New York University Press, 1961, p. 3. In many important respects Tillich's appeal to the symbolic is like Ian Ramsey's appeal to "language models," which we discuss in detail in Chapter Five.
26. Tillich, *Systematic Theology*, vol. I, pp. 152-53.

Chapter Three

On the Difficulty of Denying the Problem

T HERE HAS BEEN much discussion of meaning criteria in the past thirty years. The criteria of cognitive meaning and correct use vary considerably in strictness, so they do not all, by any means, eliminate religious assertions as meaningless. It is well known, of course, that some of them do. The interesting thing about recent responses to the problem of evil is that they reverse this strategy and make it work in favor of religion. Assuming the general meaningfulness of religious assertions they try to show that the riddle of God and evil is a pseudo-issue, resulting either from confused arguments or misused concepts. The writers who use this strategy are not applying a general meaning criterion to the problem of evil, but each finds some confusion indigenous to that specific problem. What they find amiss is always quite different. They share few philosophical predilections. They are at one only in trying to show that the problem of evil is nonsensical. That they do not succeed will be our claim. It is a claim, however, that requires a good deal of careful and detailed criticism to substantiate.

I

The problem of evil, accoiding to the first argument,[1] arises because the following two propositions are inconsistent: "God is omnipotent and no evil can be attributed to him" and "There is a state of affairs in the world which a perfectly moral Being should not tolerate." The latter proposition is based on observation. Evil has been observed in the world and this argues against belief in a theistic God. The assumption in this argument is that the problem would disappear if the universe were different than it is—that is, the problem would disappear if there were less evil, or no evil, in the world. But it can be shown that no matter how different the world might be, no matter how the world was altered, the same problem could be formulated. Since the problem violates its own assumption, it does not arise in the first place.

That altering the universe would make no difference to the problem can be shown in the following way. If present evils were reduced to a minimum, the problem would still remain because there was still some evil. If they were eliminated altogether, the problem would still remain because deprivation of positive happiness counts as evil. It is still the same if everyone were positively happy, because the fact that not everyone is happy as the happiest man would be evil. Also, it is the same if everyone were as happy as the happiest man, because the happiest man can make up an endless list of items that would increase his happiness. It is still the same if everyone were in a state of supreme satisfaction, because they all have infinite capacities for increasing their sources of satisfaction.

This part of the argument suggests a related way of pointing up the meaninglessness of the problem of evil. If the problem of evil can be solved only if God creates an infinitely happy world, then it is meaningless because it requires God to do what is logically impossible. It is just as logically impossible for him to create an infinitely happy world as it is for him to create the greatest integer.

While this argument is interesting and suggestive it quickly encounters the following fatal objections.

(A) It is true that any formulation of the problem of evil assumes that the problem would disappear if the universe were different than it is—that is, the problem would disappear if there were less, or no evil in the world. And this assumption quite clearly is justified for anything the present argument shows to the contrary. The problem of evil centers around the question of why there is apparently *gratuitous* evil in the world, not why there is any evil at all. No one would deny that some evil is necessary or desirable. Some evil may be necessary for building character, some for understanding or appreciating good by contrast, and so on. But the problem arises because no immediately obvious explanation exists to explain the necessity or desirability of all evil. Some evil is *prima facie* gratuitous. If the universe were altered to eliminate this evil while the others still remained, the problem would not arise.

(B) The core of the problem of evil is not why God did not create a perfect world but why he did not create a better one.

(C) The argument contains a shift in the meaning of *evil* without any justification of the shift. The ordinary meaning of *evil* does not include the notion of *absence of positive good*. It is understandable if a mother is grief-stricken because her child is killed, but it is not understandable if she is grief-stricken because her child is not as bright as Einstein. There may be some justification for this extension of the ordinary notion of evil, but none is given. Consequently what the argument proves is that given the extended meaning of evil, it would be logically impossible for God to remove all evil. It does not show that given the ordinary meaning of evil it would be logically impossible for God to remove all evil. But the ordinary notion, of course, is the one that both the theist and anti-theist have in mind when they are discussing the problem of evil.

(D) The argument depends upon moral assumptions which are in no way defended. That evil includes the absence of good seems doubtful on semantical grounds but that *good* is equivalent to *happiness* and that *perfect world* is equivalent to *world in which everyone is infinitely happy* seem doubtful on moral grounds. We should want to argue that there are other things good besides happiness. But in any case, the crucial point is that this dissolution of the problem of evil rests on the notion of the infinite demands of happiness. The problem of evil, however, can be formulated without any reference to happiness at all. We have stated it without reference to any particular philosophical anaylsis of the nature of *good* and *evil*. Hence any dissolution of the problem which depends upon a certain philosophical analysis of these terms is, by its very nature, inadequate.

II

The problem of evil, according to the second effort to dissolve it,[2] arises only if God is conceived to be *all*-good and *all*-powerful. If he were simply "powerful," evil could occur in spite of him. If he were simply "good," evil might occur occasionally because of him. (It is enough to call anyone good if he generally, but not always, acts benevolently.) The omnipredicates, moreover, must be interpreted descriptively if the problem is to arise. But they cannot be so interpreted. Hence the problem does not really arise in the first place. This argument is an interesting one and requires a fair amount of detail to do it justice.

The argument begins by asserting that certain ordinary predicates are comparative in nature, either explicitly or implicitly. When we say that Goliath was bigger than David, the comparison is explicit. When we say that Hercules was very strong, the comparison is implicit: We mean that he was stronger than any of the Greeks. When the omni-attributes are predicated of God, there is a similar implied comparison. Part of the meaning of *God is all-powerful* is that God is more powerful than any man, and part of the meaning of *God is all-good* is that God is morally superior to any man. This comparative analysis suggests that predicates can be ranked in the following way: *powerful, more powerful, most powerful, all-powerful*. But this suggestion is faulty. The comparative analogy breaks down eventually. The move from *most powerful* to *all-powerful* is not simply a continuation of the move from *more powerful* to *most powerful*. The latter move is legitimate but not the former. The ordinary comparative adjectives have meaning, so to speak, within boundaries or limits, but *all-powerful* cannot have all its meaning from such contexts because it is a limitless concept. Moreover, it refers to power which is different in kind from man's. God is not simply *most powerful*, but he is the very source of power itself. Finally, unlike ordinary predicates, *all-powerful* predicated of God is the Christian's way of ascribing value to him. It expresses on the part of the speaker a love of God and an acceptance of religious obligation. Hence from all angles we see that all-powerful is not like any ordinary comparative predicate (although it takes its point of departure from one of them). Hence all-powerful cannot be used descriptively. But since the riddle of God and evil depends upon its being so used, the riddle does not arise in the first place.

By way of criticism: (A) we agree that the problem of evil only arises when the omni-attributes are used. We agree that *all-powerful* gets part of its meaning from the ordinary predicate *powerful.* We agree that the comparison eventually breaks down. Being all-powerful is not simply a limiting case of man's power. But we deny that the remainder of the meaning of *all-powerful* is nondescriptive in nature. The rest of the meaning of *God is all-powerful* is that God's power extends to the capacity of doing anything which is not self-contradictory. This limitless power, so far removed from man's capacities, may well be called a power which is different in kind from man's and, in fact, the source of all power. But what is "nondescriptive" about such additional meaning? It is certainly not descriptive in the sense that it ascribes ordinary comparative properties to God—ascriptions that could be judged empirically—but it is descriptive in the sense that it imputes understandable characteristics to an unobservable entity in a completely coherent way. Since *God is all-powerful* is descriptive in this sense, and since this sort of descriptive nature is the only one necessary for stating the traditional riddle of God and evil, it follows that the riddle is not dissolved by the present argument.

(B) We agree that *God is all-powerful* might well express on the part of the speaker a love of God and a willingness to accept religious obligations. But such devotional meaning does not eliminate or change the descriptive content. Many sentences, after all, both assert a proposition and express an attitude or feeling without mutual interference. If we say that "John Smith is a busher" we may well be describing his ability along some line, but we may also be expressing our distaste for him and our unwillingness to put ourselves under obligation to him. Yet the latter function of the sentence does not eliminate or change its descriptive content. If there is no similarity between this example and the case of God's omnipotence there is nothing in the present argument that establishes this fact.

(C) If *God is all-powerful* and *God is all-good* are not descriptive expressions in any sense then they cannot be construed as expressions which are either true or false and hence cannot be construed as making any knowledge claim at all. But then a theist believes nothing which distinguishes his God from the gods of many other types of religion. That the riddle of God and evil does not arise in some of these religions we willingly admit. But to become indistinguishable from something else in order to avoid a criticism of what you are seems like too high a price to pay.

III

The problem of evil, according to a recent argument,[3] rests upon a misconception of religious morality. It depends upon the notion that *morally good* can be defined independently of *God's will*, and hence that there exists a standard by which God himself can be judged. And the judgment is that a morally perfect being would not allow evil to exist. Since there is evil, there must be no morally perfect God. The problem of evil disappears, however, upon the correct view of religious morality, namely, the view that *morally good* and *God's will* are synonymous. If divinity is the highest standard of good, then God himself cannot be legitimately judged, except in a trivial way. In fact, that there is any evil at all in the world is true only because God says so. Far from suggesting the nonexistence of God, evil, for the Christian, logically presupposes the existence of God, because it is ultimately God's will which designates what is evil in the first place. Moreover,

> If God causes or allows to exist things which are evil, i.e., which he himself condemns, then it is good for him to do so—else he wouldn't be God. Whatever God does is good, and this includes his creating things which he censures. It would therefore be absurd to argue that the existence of God is incompatible with the existence of evil—from which it follows without further argument that the Christian doctrines of God's perfection and man's need for redemption are not mutually exclusive.[4]

The success of this dissolution of the problem of evil depends, of course, upon the correctness of the analysis of religious morality upon which it rests. The following reasons are given why *morally good* should be construed as synonymous with *God's will*.

(A) To pass independent judgment upon God's actions is a straightforward abandonment of Christian morality since it is, in effect, to deny that he is *God*. After all, in such a case, some other principle would have been accepted as more fundamental than the will of God.

(B) In our civilization, and hence in our language, it would be improper to call any being God whose actions and commands were not perfectly good and moral. That God is good is a truth of language, and not a moral contingency, "since one of the usual *criteria* of Godhood is that the actions and commands of such a being are perfectly good."[5] Hence *God is the ultimate standard of good* is true by definition and to say that *God is good* becomes trivially true.

(C) It is often objected to this view that *God's will* concerns what is the case, while *morally good* concerns what ought to be the case. Since "is" statements never entail "ought" judgments, statements about God's will can never entail judgments of obligation. The reply is that belief in the Judaeo-Christian God entails normative conclusions because it presupposes a moral commitment. "In becoming a Christian theist, one commits oneself to the will of the Creator . . . as one's own highest ethical standard."[6] For Christians to be moral *is* to adhere to the will of God.

(D) Another objection to this view is that it is purely voluntaristic and hence arbitrary. "If what was good or bad as well as what ought to be done were fixed by God's will, then there could be no reason whatever for God willing in any particular way. His commands would become purely arbitrary."[7] The answer to this objection is that while there could be no *moral* obligation for God to will this rather than that, there are other considerations which guide his choice and keep it from being capricious. God is also defined as perfect in knowledge, justice, and love, and these several attributes would guide his will and choices. Such voluntaristic outcomes are anything but arbitrary.

(E) Finally it is objected that if *God is good* is trivially true, then it is unimportant and not worth asserting. The reply is that this inference from triviality is incorrect. " 'God is good' is trivially true when taken as a moral judgment, since the standard is being applied to itself, but it is not less true for that. The necessity of God's deciding amorally precludes neither his being perfectly good nor his commanding us to be nomistic by following his will."[8] The only thing that the triviality of *God is good* entails is that it tells us nothing new, nothing contingent.

To the question how do we know what the will of God is so that we have the proper standard of obligation the answer is twofold. (i) Commands can be issued directly by God through personal revelation or indirectly through scriptures and the institution of the church. (ii) One can infer by means of Natural Law the sort of thing God would command. "For we can presumably ratiocinate, at least to some degree, what a supremely intelligent, loving, and just being would will; and that is by definition what God would will, i.e., is morally binding."[9]

The directness and forcefulness of this effort to evade the problem of evil are admirable qualities and dispose one to look more kindly upon it than some of the others. But while it has freshness and boldness, it has, unfortunately for those who hold it, correspondingly harsh consequences that lead to a number of apparently insurmountable difficulties.

(A) It is rather startling to be told that this is *the* Christian viewpoint. Clearly it is not. It is not even the predominant strand in Christian thought. Most Christians have followed Augustine in the view that good is independent of God's will and hence that the evil he allows to exist requires an explanation. They have tried to explain it by producing innumerable theodicies—a vast literature which is itself a standing refutation of the claim that the present view is *the* Christian one. To act as if it is the only Christian view hides what in reality is a serious split. On this present view Augustine and all others who take the problem of evil seriously are incomplete Christians, holding, as they do, wrong-headed views of morality and God's nature, and hence in need of further conversion. No doubt the Augustinians feel the same thing is true in reverse.

(B) The argument that *God is good* is a truth of language fails to establish theological voluntarism. All it shows is that in the ordinary use of *God,* it would be inappropriate to deny the goodness of a being designated by this term. *God* is in part a moral term. However this "fact of language" is compatible with either the view that *God's will* defines *right* or that God's will is the criterion or standard of moral action because he always chooses to do what is right (where *right* is defined independently of his will).

Moreover, it is logically possible that God in fact has the usual theistic characteristics except that he is all-evil by nature and ensures the eventual defeat of goodness. The Christian, of course, would not call such a being God but then neither would anyone else. We would all refer to a Creator or use some other less neutral epithet. The important point, however, is that none of us would think of saying that such a Creator's will defined *evil*. He would be called evil because he violated our ordinary notions of right and good, which, we would hold, should, but unfortunately do not, condition his will. If this is so, it is clearly not legitimate to take God's will as defining *right* and *good* when God is conceived to be unlimited in goodness.

(C) The effort to rebut the claim that theological voluntarism is arbitrary is unsuccessful. We are told that God is also defined as perfect in knowledge, justice, and love. "He would thus by definition will in accord with these several attributes, and the result would be anything but arbitrary."[10] But the presence of the word justice here is out of place.[11] God's will presumably defines *good* and *just* and hence cannot be part of a nature that conditions a will. If it is assumed that justice does condition God's choices, then the will-of-God standard has been abandoned. The same point is true of the concept of Natural Law, which is supposedly one source for discovering what is the will of God, for Natural Law, like justice, is a normative and prescriptive term. Moreover, the notions of knowledge and love are also useless as the determiners of God's will which keep his choices from being arbitrary. Knowledge would certainly be crucial for making choices non-arbitrary, but by itself it does not constitute a motive for choice or action. Love, on the other hand, constitutes a fine motive for deciding and choosing but would reintroduce the whole problem of evil with a new terminology. How can a God un-limited in power and love permit the existence of *prima facie* gratuitous evil?

(D) The present claim is too strong. We are told not only that the will of God alone determines what is good and evil, but also that the commitment to this view must be made without reference to any prior system of morality, including our ordinary notions of good and evil. We are asked, in short, to accept "holiness" above "ordinary morality." The great danger with this view, however, is that if one gives up ordinary notions of right and wrong as providing desiderata which any ethical system must meet, at least in part, then he has given up the only standard for distinguishing between the true word of God and the numerous bogus words with which it competes.[12]

Accepting the prior validity of ordinary moral judgments does not preclude holding the will-of-God standard. We might justifiably accept the will of God as the criterion of good, as exhibiting higher wisdom, if we find it in general to uphold ordinary judgments—for which it becomes then the "ground" or justification—and to show clearly wherein they sometimes go wrong. Holding the will-of-God view in this way, however, since it involves prior moral commitments by which *God's will is determiner of good and evil* is evaluated and accepted, does not avoid the problem of evil. It is necessary to explain on this view, like any Augustinian, why in God's view something is right and good when in man's initial view it is wrong and evil.

IV

The problem of evil, still another argument goes, depends upon the confusion of treating the existence of God as an empirical question rather than one of metaphysical necessity.[13] The atheist or agnostic claims that the existence of an all-powerful and wholly good God is contradicted by the empirical fact of gratuitous evil. The comment of a logician would be, "An assertion capable of being contradicted by empirical facts is itself empirical in the broad sense, a contingent hypothesis, true if the facts happen to fit, false otherwise."[14] The argument from evil thus presupposes that theism is not a necessary truth. David Hume had great insight into this point. In his *Dialogues* he explicitly admits that if there were reason to classify theism as *a priori*, the counter argument from evil would be irrelevant. And there is good reason, of course, to classify theism (of some sort) as an *a priori* necessity. The ontological argument, e.g., establishes the existence of God as a metaphysical necessity. Anselm's argument was faulty, but he had the crucial insight. Recent arguments have corrected the faults. But the point is not simply that the ontological argument succeeds in establishing the existence of God but rather that any argument which successfully does so—and there are others—must do so by establishing the notion of God as a metaphysical necessity. There are no empirical arguments which can have any force in establishing the existence of a necessary truth like the existence of God. Likewise there can be no empirical argument against the existence of such a being. But the problem of evil is such an argument. Hence it is in principle misguided. " 'The problem of evil' is a mistake, a pseudo-problem."[15]

It is, to be sure, incredible that so many people should think that the fact of evil conflicts with theism when it is logically impossible for any empirical fact to do so. The explanation of this oddity is complex but can be summarized clearly in the following way. People had a confused, even self-contradictory, view of the meaning of *God* and, correlatively, of what is meant by *creature*, or a being other than God. God, it was held, being perfect in power, must be able to prevent everything undesirable from happening. Hence the problem of evil arose. They did not realize that this notion of omnipotence, as it figures in the riddle of God and evil, is a pseudo-idea, an absurdity. It entails the notion that God is the absolute decision maker. But this is incompatible with the notion of a creature, that is, a being other than God. Creatures have freedom, for without it there would be nothing, whether good or evil. Hence God is not the absolute decision maker and evil sometimes arises. To the question "Why is evil so much as possible?" the answer is "because a certain kind and degree of freedom makes it possible, and also makes certain good things possible, and because the chance for these good things was divinely judged worth the risk of the evil things."[16] Thus we see that "God does not adjust concrete evils and goods in some inconceivably wise way; he does not, so far as we know, manipulate concrete happenings at all. He adjusts basic kinds of possibility of good and evil as inherent in certain laws of nature. The rest is simply what the creatures happen to decide. Those who ask for a world without freedom and risk are also asking for one without opportunity. Indeed, they know not what they ask."[17]

This effort to deal with the problem of evil is an interesting combination of old ideas and new; however, as we shall see, it is no more successful than the others in avoiding the perennial pitfall of religious cosmology.

(A) The two parts of the present argument are incompatible. The first part claims that the problem of evil is a pseudo issue, while the second part offers a quasi-theistic solution to it. The claim is made that empirical evidence is irrelevant to questions about God. But many people have thought such evidence was relevant. It turns out that these "confused" people are traditional theists, while the alternative "clarification" offered is simply a quasi-theistic modification of it. Such tactics simply are not acceptable; they break the ground rules of philosophical discussion. No confusion has been demonstrated. The theist may be wrong, but he is no more confused than the quasi-theist.

The burden of the present view is that the essential freedom of beings other-than-God is incompatible with God's omniscience and omnipotence as traditionally conceived and hence that these features must be appropriately modified. But the point is this: The theist *denies* the incompatability of man's freedom and God's unlimited power and knowledge and offers *arguments* to support this position. This argument, highly refined, certainly has to be taken into account. According to the theist, God chooses to give men genuine freedom, but he in no way causes them to act the way they do. God knows, however, how they will choose even though he in no way determines that choice. There are, to be sure, difficulties with this view as we shall see when we examine the theist's free-will solution to the problem of evil, but it is not an inherently meaningless or even unclear notion and must be rebutted. Not even the beginning of a rebuttal is considered in the present argument.

(B) Rather than showing the problem of evil to be meaningless the present view in fact has its own theodicy for explaining why, even with a quasi-theistic God, there should be evil. The theodicy offered is a combination of theistic ones appropriately modified where necessary. Natural evil is explained as being inevitable results of natural laws which are on the whole good. "In setting these laws God is not decreeing this case of cancer or that case of murder; he is decreeing such and such risks of evil and such and such opportunities for good. Without the risks there could not be the opportunities, and the opportunities are divinely judged as worth the risks."[18] The freedom of creatures, with appropriate modifications in the concept of God's nature, supposedly explains moral evil. The inadequacy of both halves of this theodicy will become clear in our discussions of the natural law and free-will solutions to the problem of evil in the chapter on theism and from the whole of the chapter on quasi-theism.

(C) Unfortunately, the problem of evil envisaged in the present argument is not the crucial one. The question is seen to be one of explaining why evil is so much as possible if God is unlimited in power and goodness. The crucial problem of evil, however, is not why the world is not perfect if there is a God but rather, since some evil obviously serves good ends, why there is, nevertheless, *prima facie* gratuitous evil remaining.

(D) The first part of the present argument taken alone might be considered as a consistent argument, the burden of which is to show that the problem of evil is a pseudo-issue; in this case the argument is immediately seen to be excessively rationalistic. It claims that all empirical evidence is irrelevant to the question of whether God exists. This claim, however, is too strong even for most metaphysicians. If there were no teleological argument for the existence of God, or if—indeed—it were supremely clear, as we believe it is, that the facts of the world were incompatible with a teleological cosmology, then the reasonable conclusion to draw is that the validity of the rational arguments for the existence of God do not establish the existence of God but demonstrate the falsity of one or more of the premises.

Excessive rationalism in the past has led to strange conclusions and there seems to be no good reason for returning to such excesses. The corollary of the view that a necessary notion must be exemplified is that a self-contradictory one cannot be. Motion, space, time, and other notions have been found inconsistent by various philosophers, and hence they have denied the reality of movement, extension, and duration. They are only appearances. Most metaphysicians, hoping to avoid such paradoxical consequences, follow Kant in claiming that certain propositions about motion, space, and time are necessarily true and that the job of the metaphysician is to deduce the categorical features of mind and matter which make such truths possible. The choice between these two approaches to metaphysics can be argued indefinitely but it will depend finally to a large extent on how much respect one has for the piecemeal claims of common sense and science, on the one hand, and the claims of pure ratiocination, on the other. We have great respect for the former.

(E) The rejection of the empirical argument from evil as irrelevant has a damaging indirect consequence. If empirical facts are irrelevant then the naturalist no longer has to worry about explaining away the *prima facie* teleological aspects of the world. It cuts his task in half. He can now content himself with pointing out the deficiences of the rational arguments for the existence of God and the incompatability of the concept of a God unlimited in power and goodness with the "facts" of evil.

NOTES

1. George Schlesinger: "The Problem of Evil and the Problem of Suffering," *American Philosophical Quarterly*, I:244-47, 1964.
2. Robert E. Larsen: "The Problem of Evil and the Language of Religion," a manuscript which the author has graciously permitted us to consult prior to publication.

3. Patterson Brown: "Religious morality," *Mind, LXXII*:235-244, 1963.
4. *Ibid.*, p. 242.
5. *Ibid.*, p. 238.
6. *Ibid.*, p. 239.
7. *Ibid.*, p. 241, quotation from A. C. Ewing.
8. *Ibid.*, p. 241.
9. *Ibid.*, p. 241.
10. *Ibid.*, p. 241.
11. Antony Flew: "The 'Religious Morality' of Mr. Patterson Brown," *Mind, LXXIV*:578-81, 1965.
12. Keith Campbell: "Patterson Brown on God and Evil," *Mind, LXXIV*: 582-84, 1965.
13. Charles Hartshorne: "A New Look at the Problem of Evil," In *Current Philosophical Issues: Essays in Honor of Curt John Ducasse,* edited by F. C. Dommeyer, Springfield, Ill., Thomas, 1966, pp. 201-212.
14. *Ibid.*, p. 201.
15. *Ibid.*, p. 202.
16. *Ibid.*, p. 208.
17. *Ibid.*, p. 208.
18. *Ibid.*, p. 208.

Chapter Four

Theism I

T HE MAJORITY OF religious writers, both clerical and lay, reject evasion tactics as incompatible with theistic truth claims and believe that the problem of evil is meaningful and requires a solution. We have endeavored to show carefully why we think they are right in their beliefs. The point of the next two chapters is to examine in detail the many solutions they offer in lieu of the rejected strategies. Before beginning such an examination, however, it is only fair to say that the solutions offered vary a great deal in merit. Some are fairly simpleminded in nature and easily dismissed, while others are carefully and subtly done and require very careful attention indeed. The tradition of justifying the ways of God to man has attracted some of the greatest minds of Christendom and their efforts are not easily overturned.

The point of all the solutions offered is to show that evil is only *prima facie* gratuitous and not ultimately so. The solutions vary a great deal in nature. They may try to square evil with God's unlimited power and goodness in some strict way, or they may try to do it by "stretching" these concepts, without actually "breaking" them. Each solution is designed specifically to account for either (one type of) physical evil or moral evil; then some combination is seized upon as an adequate response to the whole problem. Our claim is that almost all of the alleged solutions account in fact for no evil at all. A few of them like the character-building solution account for a small amount and type of evil but are nothing like adequate either separately or jointly to explain the extent and types of *prima facie* gratuitous evils. It is in fact surprising how small the amount of evil is that can be justified by the few solutions that have any explanatory value at all.

It is important to be clear about the absolute inadequacy of most and the joint inadequacy of all solutions in order to avoid a fallacious argument which the theist sometimes relies upon if he becomes convinced that all theodicies have faults. While admitting the faults, he says that this is no cause for despair. He argues that theodicies operate like a case of converging evidence in a court of law. No piece of circumstantial evidence is sufficient to establish that X is the case or that X occurred, but all the pieces taken together do converge toward this conclusion. So it is with solutions to the problem of evil. None is sufficient to establish the fact that *prima facie* gratuitous evil is not genuinely gratuitous, but all of them taken together converge toward that conclusion.

This sort of tactic, however, is completely spurious. It has been called appropriately the Ten-leaky-buckets-Tactic.[1] It amounts to saying that while one cannot carry water far in a leaky bucket with ten of them he can. The reason the analogy to converging evidence breaks down is because every item of evidence in such a case has some weight in its own right while in the case of the Ten-leaky-buckets-Tactic every argument either holds no water at all, or in a few cases, such a little amount as to be useless.

I

We shall consider the large number of candidates which have been offered as solutions to physical evil in the present section and the ones offered as solutions to moral evil in the next. While we do not consider all the solutions which have ever been advanced, we do consider all the major ones, the ones taken most seriously by theists themselves.

(A) Evil is necessary as a contrast, one argument goes, so that sentient beings will be able to understand and properly appreciate the nature of good. One learns what *good* means, and appreciates it as good by experiencing the contrast between it and evil, just as one learns what the color red is by experiencing the contrast between it and other colors.

This view has the merit of being straightforward, but it encounters immediate difficulties. (i) It is not an adequate justification of all physical evil as it is represented to be. It is in fact directed only at the problem of pain—one of the problems of physical evil, to be sure, but not synonymous with it. Insanity does not necessarily entail pain but the deprivation involved is clearly to be classified as a physical evil. (ii) Even as far as the problem of pain is concerned the contrast solution breaks down. We need little pain by way of contrast to get the point: One might be allowed to bite his lip occasionally rather than have cancer of the mouth. (iii) Moreover, it is doubtful that the underlying principle of this argument is valid. It entails the view that if a person who had never experienced pleasure became infected with tetanus he would not understand and appreciate the pain involved. But this consequence is absurd. "It is true that it might not be distinguished by a special name and called 'pain,' but the state we now describe as a painful state would nonetheless be possible in the total absence of pleasure." In addition, "the converse would seem to apply. Plato brings this out very clearly in Book 9 of the *Republic* in respect of the pleasures of taste and smell. These pleasures seem not to depend for their existence on any prior experience of pain."[2]

√(B) Evil, many writers have suggested, is a necessary by-product of the laws of our universe, laws which produce on the whole beneficial results. God, of course, being unlimited in power, could have created any world he chose. What he did was to create a world with laws that would produce overall good results although calamitous in some particular effects. Having created the one he did it would be irrational to expect him constantly to suspend its laws by miraculous intervention to prevent specific evils. Besides, such intervention would both undercut our moral fiber and make nature so irregular as to make the use of our reason impossible.

Against this argument the following objections can be urged. (i) It is clearly limited in its explanation of physical evil. Not all disease can be explained along these lines. (ii) A God unlimited in power and goodness certainly could have created a world with somewhat different laws than the present ones which would have produced much the same good results and avoided much of the gratuitous evil. God, for example, could have produced the same results in the biological world with the same mechanism of natural selection but without its present fantastic wastefulness. This could be done, e.g., by assuring a larger percentage of favorable mutations. (iii) If it is possible for God to interfere miraculously to avoid a gratuitous evil, then it would seem to be unreasonable and evil for him *not* to do so in some particularly hideous cases. Some theists try to avoid this difficulty by saying God is not able to interfere with his creation once completed. This maneuver, however, abandons traditional theism because it relinquishes the notion that God is unlimited in power.

(iv) It is not at all clear that God's intervention would undercut moral fiber. Anthropological studies indicate that belief in the possibility of divine intervention in deserving cases tends not to undercut our moral fiber, but rather to "provide an incentive for moral life . . . [and] also strengthen our wills against adversity."[3] Of course it might be argued that too much intervention would eventually lead to reduction of moral fiber. However, to show that this solution of the problem of physical evil fails we need only show that *occasional* intervention could be expected of an omnipotent and all-good God. And this is not difficult to do.[4]

(v) F. R. Tennant's argument that God should never intervene because intervention would make the world so unpredictable that we could not operate rationally is untenable because it is like arguing that one should never take two aspirin because taking two hundred would be fatal.[5] Certainly if God always interfered with the regularities of nature in order to avoid terrible consequences he would produce a complete breakdown of predictability and chaos would result. But it is quite clear that he could occasionally abridge regularities to avoid particularly disastrous results without introducing the slightest chaotic element.

The by-product solution is perhaps most urgently needed in dealing with animal pain. Since many other arguments obviously will not work with animals (e.g., suffering cannot be punishment to creatures who are not morally responsible) many fall back on the view that the apparently brutal laws of nature make possible the survival of the fittest and consequently the development of species which is in the long run to the betterment of the animal kingdom.[6] "If all animals had been herbivorous and healthy, they would mostly starve as a result of their own multiplication."[7]

The chief difficulty with this explanation of animal pain is that it assumes that God could not have chosen another birthrate. To be sure, God could not have chosen another birthrate and still have expected natural selection in its present form to work, but God was not obliged to adopt the present fantastically wasteful mechanism of natural selection.[8] There are many ways in which God could have saved an enormous amount of suffering by altering the mechanism of evolution. For example, he could have seen to it that a larger percent of mutations are favorable. As it is now, advantageous mutations are a minute percentage.

Farrer misunderstands the whole issue of animal pain. "The issue we have to consider," he writes, "lies in the simple question whether animals would be better off, if they had no pains at all."[9] This is precisely what the issue is not. We are not asking whether animals could do nicely without any pain at all but rather whether at least *some* of their pain is not gratuitous in the sense that God could have altered the mechanism of evolution in such a way that its working entailed much *less* suffering.

Tennant and many other theists have insisted that some set of general laws must be sacrosanct in the world, but the alteration we have suggested would not require intervention in particular cases but merely less wasteful general laws of evolution.

(C) The argument that evil is punishment for sin was advanced by Job's comforters. They were surprised that Job had so successfully hidden his sins from men's eyes, but since he was punished he must of necessity have sinned secretly. We know, of course, from the very structure of the Book of Job, that this interpretation of evil is wrong as far as this document is concerned. Job, as God knew, had *not* done anything to merit his misery; the point of his suffering lay elsewhere. Indeed, Christ himself apparently rejected the view that evil is simply punishment for sin. In any case, this retribution solution is quite untenable on any ground, Christian or otherwise. Consider the Peru landslides which annihilated many men, women, and children of several valley villages. If evil is punishment for sin, it is difficult to believe that only the inhabitants of these villages deserved such reprimands. Moreover, as Voltaire observed, it is difficult to believe that just the sinners get singled out for destruction in such catastrophes.

W. H. Sheldon has suggested that it is at least possible that sufferings undeserved by deeds in this life are punishment for evil deeds in an earlier incarnation.[10] This suggestion, however, is not very helpful even if we were to take the reincarnation hypothesis seriously. Even as a mere possibility the hypothesis provides only temporary relief because it immediately has the problem of explaining the original moral evil. We ask at once why God permitted all the moral evil in earlier incarnations for which we are now being punished, and we will show later in this chapter that all explanations for the amount of moral evil in the world fail. Among the further more obvious difficulties in the reincarnation hypothesis is the one of why God has systematically deluded Christians about why he is punishing them. Such delusion hardly argues for the existence of a God unlimited in goodness.

(D) God tests people like Job, it is said, precisely because he knows they will be steadfast in their faith and thus act as a salutary example to other people. Unfortunately, this solution is more vulnerable than any other. Not everyone is a Job, and when affliction causes renunciation of God this makes a very bad example for fellow Christians. Moreover such an interpretation could not account for mass disasters and catastrophes. In such cases people do not remain steadfast in faith and act as good examples for others. They simply disappear off the face of the earth.

✓(E) The view that physical evil is God's "warning" to man is a clear and straightforward one, and it is particularly dear to the heart of a practical theist. Men are sunk, he says, in religious indifference, and they need to be shocked into realization of God's presence by some awesome display of his power. When natural catastrophes like earthquakes, floods, and tornadoes occur, men become aware of God's great power, and their own littleness in the face of it; they take on, as a result, the proper reverential awe of the Creator and a fear of violating his laws. These moral and religious results, in short, justify the physical pain resulting from natural causes. But do they? It is clear enough to anyone except a practical theist that they do not. God's demonstration of power, after all, need not be so deadly to achieve its aim, if this aim could be achieved at all. But it is certain that its aim, in fact, is not achieved. Indeed, rather than bringing man to God, these natural calamities frequently turn men against him. Such calamities forcefully bring to man's attention the whole problem of evil, and this problem, so difficult to solve, causes many people to give up their religious beliefs rather than strengthening them. According to a recent commentator, "if God's object in bringing about natural calamities is to inspire reverence and awe, He is a bungler."[11] Moreover, "the use of physical evil to achieve this object is hardly the course one would expect a benevolent God to adopt when other, more effective, less evil methods are available to Him, for example, miracles, special revelation, etc."[12]

(F) Leibniz's theodicy is extremely important, but his claim that "this is the best of all possible worlds" is open to misunderstanding. *This is the best of all possible worlds* can be interpreted to mean that this is the best of all logically possible worlds. This interpretation is equivalent to saying that the world is perfect, that evil is only an illusion. It can also be interpreted to mean that this is the best world that it was possible for God to create. On this interpretation evil is not an illusion but a real ingredient of the world. The point is that it contains the minimum amount of evil that was compatible with the creation of any world at all.

The ambiguity in this claim has led to the traditional misinterpretation of Leibniz's theodicy. He is misinterpreted as making the former claim, when in fact he is making the latter one. For Leibniz this is the best of all possible worlds, even though evil is a necessary ingredient of it. It is logically impossible for any finite thing to be perfect; hence it is impossible even for God to create a perfect world. The very act of creation entails imperfection or evil. This is what Leibniz meant by *metaphysical evil*. God's genius, however, lies in the fact that he created the world with the least amount of necessary evil in it. The amount of evil in the world, in short, is just right commensurate with there being any world at all.

Any criticism of Leibniz has two parts. First, one can criticize the notion of metaphysical evil. Why cannot a theistic God create a perfect world? A theistic God, after all, is supposed to be all-powerful not only *within* nature but *over* nature as well.[13] Thus God could have created any world he wished, and could have chosen to create a perfect one. The problem centers around what one means by *perfect*. If one means by *perfect world* a world infinitely better than the present one, then God indeed could not create a perfect world. But if one means by *perfect world* a world in which there is no positive evil, then God could certainly create such a perfect world, because the concept is not a self-contradictory one. In any case, even if God could not create a perfect world in the second sense, the problem remains why he should have created any world at all if he could not create one better than the present world. This is the poignant burden of Ivan's question to Alyosha: If you were God, would you have consented to create the present world if its creation depended upon the unexpiated tears of one tortured child crying in its stinking outhouse to "dear, kind God"? The answer to this question, no doubt, is that God is not "man writ large." A terrifying result of this answer is to make one wonder what such a God *would* be like.

Second, one can challenge the claim that this world has the minimum amount of evil in it commensurate with the existence of any world at all. A world with any evil at all in it meets Leibniz's requirements of the inevitability of metaphysical evil. To answer the question why the world needed to have as much evil as it does, one needs to say that just the present amount was required to cultivate courage, patience, self-sacrifice, and so on. This is the most incredible part of the Leibnizian view, and it is the part that has led to its misidentification with the view that evil is only an illusion. The sufficient answer here is that no effort to explain why the nature and amount of evil in this world is necessary is successful. Some evil always remains gratuitous and a reproach to a theistic God. Moreover, it is not just the nature and amount of evil that causes the theist trouble; the distribution of it also constitutes a problem. That some people live in agony while others prosper hardly seems like the "right" amount of evil. The fact that good and evil consequences so often fail to fit the deserts of the people on whom they fall further complicates matters.

Nels Ferré[14] has tried recently to justify the unjust distribution of evil in the following way: God needed an order in which good and bad consequences were distributed generally, and not always according to merit, so that the social nature of man, including compassion, sympathy, and the ability to experience life vicariously, might be developed. But this justification simply will not do, because it is quite possible to develop an individual's sense of dependence on the community without such extensive vicarious reward and punishment as exists in our world.

The argument here is related to that of some famous schoolmasters who have held that punishing the whole class for the misdeeds of one member is for the good of every boy's character —making him feel part of a community. However, it is perfectly possible to develop a child's social nature in a less harsh manner —perhaps even by group sports. The theist often assumes that either the desirable end must be achieved by the existing (extremely painful) means or not at all, when in fact it is possible to use alternative (less painful, if not entirely painless) means.

✓(G) The "ultimate harmony" solution is ambiguous; there are in fact two separate positions which usually have this name. There is the claim that "all's well in God's view," and the claim that "all's well that ends well." Both views have been extremely influential.

All's well in God's view. It is this claim which is usually introduced by musical metaphors. Just as a chord when heard in isolation may sound dissonant but when heard in context sounds harmonious, so it is with evil: An event seen in isolation is called evil by man, but this event seen in relation to all other events is called good by God. This analogy should not be interpreted as suggesting that there are two ways of judging events—

man's and God's—and that each one is perfectly valid in its own way. Rather the point of the analogy is that God's way is really correct and man's way incorrect. Whenever man judges that "X is evil," he is mistaken; whatever man ordinarily calls evil is not evil after all. In God's higher morality evil is only an illusion.

The objections to this claim are numerous, but several of them are particularly damaging. (i) If there really is no evil in the world, then any efforts to remove *prima facie* evil are necessarily morally wrong. Any reform movement is by its very nature pernicious. This result seems like a *reductio ad absurdum* of the present view; yet it is quite clear that this view is the (usually implicit) bridge which many people use to cross the chasm between their Christian beliefs and their extreme *laissez-faire* political views.[15] (ii) The fact that God would permit men to be deceived systematically would itself constitute the most staggering evil that he could have permitted.

(iii) The most fundamental criticism is that the concept of God's higher morality has no meaning whatever. If God's higher morality is completely different from man's ordinary moral notions, then this higher morality is completely meaningless, since man has no other notions of good and evil except the ordinary ones. Consequently, when a theist says that he accepts God's higher morality, this claim of acceptance is vacuous. The only way for him to avoid this allegation is to claim that while man's and God's morality are not the same, nevertheless there are metaphorical or analogical bridges which help him "make the crossing" to the new meanings. However, such efforts are doomed to fail because the lacuna between man's morality and God's higher morality is absolute. The acceptance of God's higher morality entails the falsity of *every* claim that X is evil. Consequently it entails the pointlessness of *every* correlative claim that X is good. But if all ordinary judgments of evil and good are either necessarily false or pointless, then clearly they contain no analogical bases for understanding God's higher morality. Hence, again, the theist's claim that he accepts God's higher morality is, of necessity, vacuous. His claim is not false; it simply does not make any sense.

(iv) The concept of a higher morality implied by the ulti-

mate harmony view requires further comment. J. S. Mill re-
nounced this notion in the following way. He said, in effect:
In everyday life I know what to call right or wrong, because I
can plainly see its rightness or wrongness. Now if a god requires
that what I ordinarily call wrong in human behavior I must
call right when he does it; or that what I ordinarily call wrong
I must call right because he so calls it, even though I do not
see the point of it; and if by refusing to do so, he can sentence
me to hell, to hell I will gladly go.[16]

Theists have argued against Mill in the following way.
Consider the moral relations between a father and son. Certainly
a father knows moral principles of action that are unknown to
his son. Now would it not be presumptuous for a son to say to
his father that he could not accept as right anything of which
he did not plainly see the rightness. Would it not be presumptuous to say, "Father, rather than call right what you call right—
which I cannot, since this is not what I mean by right—I would
be willing to go to hell." Theists suggest that there is certainly
as much difference between man and God as there is between
a child and his father. This analogy, we believe, is not very
convincing. We need to make the parallel more exact.[17] The
child rightly has faith in his father's wisdom about things
unknown to him. But the point is this: The child infers this
wisdom from the wisdom and goodness of his father which he
has seen and understood. He is, in short, as in all areas of
thought, reasoning from the known to the unknown. With God,
however, the case is quite different. We are asked to accept
a higher morality out of devotion and total ignorance. Indeed,
the only thing we do know about it is that it runs counter
to all that we *have* seen and understood about right and wrong.
We are asked, in effect, to forget the little we know of right
and wrong, abdicate our intelligence, submit ourselves to something we know not of—all this out of blind devotion to the
God about whom we have to raise serious questions! If a child
followed such a course of action toward his father, we would not
think it an act of deep filial piety at all, but one of abject
submission. The same attitude ought to exist, we submit, in the
case of God and man.

All's well that ends well. The second view that comes under the heading "ultimate harmony" is this: Man, seeing only short run consequences, fails to understand that present evils eventually lead to important goods. God, however, seeing long run consequences, understands that they are good enough to compensate for, or make worthwhile, the evils along the way. God, of course, arranged that it should be so. This view does *not* entail the claim that evil is only an illusion. It claims that evil is justified by the long run, not that the concept disappears because of it.

What can be said against this view? There are numerous objections, as we shall see, but we might well begin by asking for an example of how present evil is compensated for by future good. We have been astounded through the years by the examples offered: Indeed we have become convinced there is nothing that someone cannot find to be ultimately justified. We once mentioned Buchenwald as an example of great moral evil. But it was ultimately useful, someone suggested, because it had helped immeasurably in solving the problem of population explosion. We were agitated and offered to shovel the speaker into our furnace as an added good. The important point here is that if one holds the present view and honestly goes into detail trying to discover the future good, he gets really bizarre results. Hence, the person who holds this view wisely refrains from offering detailed analyses. He contents himself with saying simply that in all cases there is an ultimate good, known to God, which human beings with their limited powers are unable to fathom.

There are at least four serious objections to the claim that all's well that ends well. (i) Even if it should be true that all short run evils produce long run goods, all this would prove is that the world is less evil than it would be if short run evils also produced long run evils. It would not explain why God permits the short run evils to exist. Could he not have produced the same results with less ghastly short run evils? (ii) The price that is paid for long run good is too high; the incredible amount of misery endured by sentient beings, and its unjust distribution, ruins the value of any possible goals. The end does not justify the means. The notion that all's well that ends well ignores the wounds along the way. Some will never heal. A selection to read here is "Pro and Contra" from the *Brothers Karamasov*. No doubt, on the day of resurrection, Ivan says, I too will join the chorus, "Hallelujah, God, thy ways are just!" I too shall sing, as the mother embraces her son's murderer, "Praise God, I see why it had to be!" But, he concludes, I loath myself now for the very thought of doing that then. I renounce the ultimate harmony altogether, while I still can, while there is still time. For the love of man I now renounce it altogether.

(iii) The concept of the long run itself is not without difficulty. We see cases where evil events produce good consequences in the long run. But we also see cases where evil events only produce more evil consequences in the long run. If it be objected that we have not waited long enough in the latter cases, then the question arises of how long the long run is. Either the theist gives no answer or else depends upon the tautological one that the long run coincides with the appearance of good consequences. The problem of the long run, to be sure, appears in various philosophical contexts, but it appears in a peculiarly difficult form in the present one. What we have in mind is this. The frequency advocate runs into the same problem of the long run in probability theory. The a priori theorist accuses him of a tautological criterion of the long run. By way of defense the frequentist offers the concept of mathematical limit as an independent criterion of the long run. There are still difficulties with this view, but at least he has produced an independent criterion. The trouble with the theist's view that all's well that ends well, however, is that by its very nature, his long run cannot be defined in any way except a tautological one.

(iv) The present view, unlike the claim that all's well in God's view, is a perfectly meaningful one. It is possible and hence understandable that God arranged the world so that present evils always result in long run goods—where evil and good have their ordinary denotations. The odd thing, however, is that the theist seems to think that if it is *possible* God so arranged things, it is *probable* that he did. This conclusion seems odd because ordinarily we do not go from the possibility of something to its probability. We only go from the possibility to the probability because we have some evidence to bridge the gap. The theist, however, is not troubled by the lack of evidence. Already believing in God, he thinks that if a certain possible arrangement of events would solve the problem of evil, then it is not only probable but certain that God so arranged them. The theist, we believe, has a perfectly good right to ignore the lack of positive evidence and to bridge the gap anyway. But he does not have the right to ignore the evidence that tends to show the possible in this case is unlikely and to bridge the gap nevertheless. The previous points, we believe, provide the required negative evidence and hence make the theist's usual bridging of the gap untenable.

There is, finally, what might be called a wholesale version of the all's-well-that-ends-well doctrine that deserves brief mention. According to this view, immortality sufficiently compensates for whatever evil happens to a person in this life. Eternal bliss is thought capable of making worthwhile any amount of suffering along the route to that goal. However, the afterlife argument is far from convincing because it is very much like a torturer telling his victim on the rack that he need not be concerned for by and by he will be sent to a luxurious spa. To be sure, the victim is delighted to hear that he has such a future ahead of him, but he still cannot understand why he need be tortured before he goes. He cannot understand why the one should be a prerequisite for the other. The torture remains gratuitous for anything the spa argument shows to the contrary.

✓(H) According to St. Augustine, evil has no being itself, but is only the absence of good. Being itself is always good, and evil occurs only as the corruption of a substance. In the *Enchiridion* he wrote,

> For what is that which we call evil but the absence of good? In the bodies of animals, disease and wounds mean nothing but the absence of health; for when a cure is effected, that does not mean that the evils which were present—namely, the diseases and wounds— go away from the body and dwell elsewhere: they altogether cease to exist; for the wound or disease is not a substance, but a defect in

the fleshy substance—the flesh itself being a substance, and therefore something good of which those evils—that is, privations of the
good which we call health—are accidents.[18]

However effective this analysis of evil might be as a defense
against the early dualistic heresy in Christianity, for which
purpose Augustine used it, it is completely useless by itself for
solving the problem of evil. In the words of a recent commentator,

You have not made the world out any better, in saying it is spoilt
by its own anarchy and decay, rather than by adulteration with a
dark element, foreign to its nature. If the milkman brings us curdled
milk, we may not greatly care whether he has dropped acid into it,
or simply let it turn bad; either way it is undrinkable. St. Augustine
has not eased the problem of evil, or exculpated God. He has merely
defended the single origin of the world.[19]

This being the case, we need not enter into a discussion of the
merits of the Augustinian theory of being and nonbeing.

However, the Neoplatonic notion that any substance is good
entails the principle of plenitude, and this principle, as used by
Augustine, does constitute a possible answer to the problem
of physical evil. Austin Farrer has used this principle in an
interesting way in his own recent theodicy and demonstrates
that there is still very much life in the Augustinian tradition.[20]

According to Farrer, the grand cause of physical evil is the
mutual interference of systems, both physical and organic. Everything, in just being itself, interferes of necessity with the free
movement of other systems and in turn is interfered with. Such
mutual trouble is indigenous to any world which has genuine
natural forces and living creatures and is not simply a celestial
machine. To rid the world of such evil would be to get rid of
the world, and any possible other one, not to create an ideal one.

Physical evil, of course, could be avoided if God chose not
to create any world at all. The question then arises why, in
spite of the necessity of physical evil attendant upon any creation, God nevertheless created. It is essentially a hopeless enter-
prise to try to answer this question, Farrer says, since divine
decision is hopelessly beyond the range of human conceiving.
But the answer, he continues, may lie along the following lines
(and here it is that he uses the principle of plenitude). God

desires the existence of creatures that shall be excellent. Not simply ones of the highest excellence, however, since God already fills this category. "To realize the divinest good, he has not to create, but to live. But there are lower levels of excellence possible; and it is better they should be filled, than lie empty."[21] Thus it is that God creates all the substances of the universe including physical ones. At this point, however, Farrer observes, another problem arises. Why should God create the physical world and all its creatures with its necessary evil when he could have satisfied his creative inclinations wholly within the spiritual realm. Certainly God's infinite inventiveness could devise endless numbers of new kinds of spiritual beings. Why descend from the highest altitude? The answer is that God desired to create beings able to know and love him. Spiritual substance is simply a reflection of God himself and hence not something other than himself which could know and love him. So God created the physical world with its strong animal minds that could aspire to know and love him in spite of their native physicality. "It seems a disappointing conclusion, and quite unworthy of the Creator's wisdom," Farrer writes, but this is not surprising "since in presuming to reason as we do, we are guided by our own reason, not by his."[22]

This contemporary version of ancient views, even though refreshingly different from most other theistic strategy, encounters problems of equal magnitude.

(i) While Farrer presents a rational theodicy he enters reservations. "Divine decision is hopelessly beyond the range of human conceiving." "It seems a disappointing conclusion, and quite unworthy of the Creator's wisdom." And so on. These reservations reveal Farrer's presuppositions. God exists so there must be some point to evil. We can always rely on that. With that understood, we can try to satisfy our rational nature by guessing what the point of it is. If we fail to satisfy our rational nature that, of course, is no cause for despair. This attitude, however, as we have seen, is impossible for a theist. It misses the essential point that if he does not have a genuine answer to the problem of evil he has no right to say that he *knows* that God exists.

(ii) We agree that any possible universe entails some mutual interference and hence some evil. We agree that it is impossible to create a universe without any evil. But it is clear that there are many possible universes other than the present one with much less interference and much less evil which God could have created. The crucial question arises why he did not do so since he is presumably unlimited in power and goodness. Moreover, if God is unlimited in power as the theist claims, then he should be able to impose a more just distribution of evils no matter which possible system of mutual interference he chose to create.

(iii) The principle of plenitude has a fatal deficiency. It depends upon the notion that substance itself is necessarily good or valuable. This view binds together in a necessary relationship existential and value concepts. Existence implies value. Thus the denial that existence is a value should be a self-contradictory claim. Yet there have been many Indian and Oriental philosophers and Western philosophers like Schopenhauer who have interpreted being and substance as evil and look upon non-existence as the ultimate value to be achieved. These philosophies have their deficiences, no doubt, but they are no more clearly self-contradictory than Neoplatonism. Since the denial of the value of existence is not self-contradictory we conclude that there is only a contingent relationship between existence and value terms. Existence is not necessarily related to either value or disvalue. They are separate notions, and given different value systems different estimates of the value of being will be made. That existence and value are separate notions, of course, is also the common-sense view of the matter. Hence solutions to the problem of evil which depend upon the principle of plenitude are usually viewed with suspicion.

(iv) There are two parts of Farrer's theodicy which do not fit together well. According to Farrer, it is good that all possible spots in creation should be filled. Yet it is the mutual interference that results thereby which causes the great amount of physical evil in the world. These two notions, if not outright incompatible, certainly produce paradoxical results. It entails the notion that the more evil we have the better! The only way to avoid this paradox is to accept another Augustinian view, namely, that what appears to be evil is in reality good. Evil is like an ugly patch that makes a whole picture more beautiful than it would be without it. This view, sometimes called the "aesthetic" view of evil, is synonymous with the first version of what is called the ultimate harmony solution, and the deficiencies of this sort of approach already have been analyzed in detail.

(v) Finally, to say that God would create a physical world with all its creatures so that he could be known and loved seems extremely unconvincing. Presumably no species but man can know and love God. Why the other competing systems? Is it pious and still within the Christian tradition to ascribe the needs of understanding and love to God? Is it commensurate with the higher morality of God that the satisfaction of his desires justify the countless agonies of sentient beings? Farrer is right in drawing back from this solution. Whatever wisdom God might see in allowing evil to exist, certainly it could not be for the satisfaction of his own needs and desires.

(I) The character-building solution has had a long and continuous history. It has been held recently by the English philosophical theologians F. R. Tennant and William Temple "and can be traced through Schleiermacher in the nineteenth century back to some of the early Hellenistic Fathers of the Christian Church, especially Irenaeus."[23] According to this view, the rough edges of the world are necessary for producing spiritually significant beings. In a world without tears there would be no occasion for the production of courage, endurance, charity, and sympathy. Such a world would not miss them since it would have no need for them. Such an Arcadian world might seem good in prospect but in fact would be very bland. It would be much less desirable than a world that had both evil and the greatness of spiritual growth.

One must admit that this view is an attractive one. Who has not had the experience of wishing fervently to avoid some painful or even harrowing event and yet, after the event, had to admit that he is a better person for having undergone it? The difficulties with this view, however, are simple, clear, and utterly damaging. (i) This solution is simply inapplicable to some physical evils, insanity being perhaps the best example. (ii) At best it can only account for a small amount of evil and cannot account at all for the maiming of character which too much evil often produces (consider the brainwashing cases) or the mass annihilation of character (recall the Peru landslides). (iii) The price that is paid for spiritual growth even when it does occur is often too high to be justly exacted. (iv) Moreover, it is not clear why God, if he is all-powerful, could not have created spiritually significant people in the first place. The answer here supposedly is this: It is just as logically impossible for God to create a spiritually significant being who never experienced sorrow or suffering as it is for him to create a table that is black and white all over at the same moment.[24] This answer is plausible as far as certain virtues are concerned. It would be absurd to expect courage in a world where nothing was frightening, or patience in a world without painful delays, or charity where there was no neediness, and so on. But these negative virtues certainly do not exhaust the spiritual realms. "Neither all moral goodness nor the highest moral goodness is triumph in the face of adversity or benevolence towards others in suffering. Christ Himself stressed this when he observed that the two great commandments were commandments to love. Love does not depend for its possibility on the existence and conquest of evil."[25] (v) If courage, endurance, charity, sympathy, and the like are so spiritually significant, then the evil conditions which foster them should not be mitigated. Social and political reforms designed to achieve social security, peace, plenty, and harmony automatically become pernicious. We do not really believe this, of course, and thereby reflect the fact that we have spiritual values which we place above those negative ones fostered by extremely trying conditions.

II

The problem of moral evil poses a two-way difficulty for the theist. Moral evil entails both the debasement of character and the infliction of enormous amounts of suffering on fellow creatures. Why does God permit such self-damaging and other-damaging behavior?

Theists have only two major types of solutions to the problems of moral evil. One depends upon the specific concepts of a historical religion, namely, Christianity, and the other, the free-will solution, is endorsed universally among theists.

(A) According to one version of the Christian tradition man is sinful by nature and deserves eternal punishment.[26] However, Jesus, the Incarnation of God upon earth, suffered and died on the cross in order to atone for man's sinfulness and to redeem him from his justly deserved eternal punishment.

The difficulties with this view are so numerous that it has long since ceased being a dominant tradition even in Protestant Christianity. The first point to notice is that the doctrines of the Incarnation, Atonement, and Redemption, even if true, have no value whatever in solving the problem of evil. Even if true, they would provide only a grateful release from suffering but would not begin to explain the need for it in the first place. No doubt one should be grateful for being rescued from an intolerable situation, but being rescued does not explain why one was subjected to it in the first place. There is a vast difference between gratitude for precious improvement in one's ghastly lot and an explanation of why it was no better to begin with. Hence, the only part of this argument which has any relevance to the problem of evil is the claim that evil is punishment for sins. However, we have seen previously the hopeless deficiencies of this claim. But this version of it has even further difficulties. It throws serious doubt on the unlimited goodness of God to say that he created finite beings who are evil by nature and reap eternal punishment. Moreover, if human beings are evil by nature— that is, have no chance of freely choosing between good and evil—then it makes no sense to say that they deserve punishment. The difficulties of the present view proved so great that the bulk of Protestant theologians returned to the long-standing, free-will solution, or some modern variation thereof, the nature of which, and attendant difficulties, we will examine soon.

There is, however, another uniquely Christian approach to the problem which is currently in favor. According to some Christian theologians the problem can be met by encountering "the Event" of Christ's birth, crucifixion, and resurrection which is "God's seal on evil's doom."[27]

> 'Jesus [was] killed by the hands of lawless men. But God raised him up, having loosed the pangs of death' [*Acts* 2: 23-24]. So his first followers had for their joy this mighty demonstration of God's power and will.[28]

We are not given any explanation, but we are given a victory.[29] We are not told by God what the *nature* of providence is, but we are unmistakably shown by God in the Event that *some* such providence (i.e. ultimate harmony in God's view) exists. Although the mystery is ineradicable, this historical fact demonstrates conclusively that evil and pain "have been under control from 'the foundation of the world'."[30] In our knowledge of this historical fact we existentially *encounter* this control, these theologians maintain, even though we cannot hope to explain that control. "Sin, hatred, physical agony, premature death, the innocent suffering for the guilty" are all unmistakably encountered as meaningful in Christ's life and this clearly indicates that they are meaningful (albeit mysteriously) in every human life.[31]

This solution, impressive in its boldness, is a variant of a general strategy discussed in Chapter One. The general strategy is to say that the religious man has various grounds for believing in God—existential, historical, and rational—and thus knowing that God exists, he knows that there is no genuine gratuitous evil in the world, that God has some purpose in all evil even though we do not know what it is. The present argument simply stresses the notion of "existential encounter" and "historical events of a uniquely Christian sort." The same criticisms that apply to the general strategy apply in part to this variant of it. (i) The existential grounds of belief are admittedly important and not to be ignored. However, there are existential grounds which pull the other way for those initially sensitive to the suffering of others or those who become sensitive through discussions of the problem of evil. The real trouble for some people is that competing existential demands pull them painfully in opposite directions. Clearly there are considerations other than existential ones, then, that must help decide the issue. (ii) To encounter the Event supposedly allows us to say that we *know* that God exists and that he triumphs over evil. However, in order to say that he *knows* that God exists and triumphs over evil, the Christian must not simply be certain of being right and happen in fact to be right, but he must have evidence adequate to warrant his degree of confidence. And he does not have adequate evidence when he ignores the fact that Christian doctrine has grave difficulty in making sense of evil. Unless this difficulty is removed, the Christian cannot say that he *knows* that God exists and triumphs over evil.

Moreover, the present version of the argument has difficulties uniquely its own. (iii) A problem hinges on precisely what is contained in the historical Event. Let us assume that the resurrection is a genuine historical fact, that someone named Jesus died and came alive again. As a matter of historical fact we have before us only the return of life, and the *connection* between the resurrection and the regular habits of a hypothetical power responsible for this resurrection is not a matter of historical fact. The historical event contains only the return of life, not a piece, so to speak, of the alleged ultimate harmony.

(iv) Much of the apparent strength of the argument is the result of begging the question. It is argued that Jesus did not merely die and come alive again; he atoned for our sins, he is the pivotal point of history, and so on. Unfortunately, these additional descriptions of Jesus' life are not based on the bare historical facts, but constitute an interpretation which presupposes the ultimate harmony, and it is just this ultimate harmony that is in question.

(v) Finally, the erroneous assumption is made that the suffering in everyone's life can have as beneficial effects on other people as Christ's suffering has had. Theologians can point to the great comfort which countless people have found in knowing that Christ suffered even more than they are suffering. In innumerable ways Christ's life has given meaning to the lives of others, and consequently, it is argued, it seems fair to say that Christ's suffering was in no way gratuitous. If Christ's intense agony was not gratuitous, then why should we consider other people's suffering gratuitous.

However, one could grant that *Christ's* suffering paid fantastic dividends in human welfare without supposing that the suffering of others must have such beneficial effects. Millions have suffered quite obscure agony from which only a few (if any) close associates derived any benefit.

(B) Theists of all shades and varieties rely upon some version of the free-will solution as the most fundamental approach to the problem of moral evil.[32] One version is this: God, being omniscient, knew that man would willfully choose the wrong sometimes if he had free will; but God granted him free will anyway because not to do so would have produced greater evil. A world with only robots in it would be less good than a world with freely choosing men who sometimes rebel against morality.

There are, however, several trying problems for this version of the free-will solution. (i) God could have created a world in the first place where free will when misused would not produce such disastrous consequences as in the present one. (ii) God could have avoided the more ghastly consequences of misused freedom by creating man with a *disposition* to act rightly even though he might choose occasionally to do evil. The latter is all that would be required for the possibility of man's freedom and moral rebellion. Yet God did not do this. Such behavior seems to argue against either all-powerfulness or all-goodness. It is insufficient for the theist to reply that God did not create man with a tendency to act rightly because this would preclude the moral growth attendant upon struggle in the face of great odds. This reply misses the point that great evil, rather than causing growth, often stunts and destroys the free human soul.[33] God, on this view, is doing this dreadful thing apparently: He creates human beings with free will, some of whom will grow spiritually through great evil, and some of whom will be destroyed completely. How can the former justify God's way in view of the latter? The price is too high to pay. Indeed, this whole view goes contrary to ordinary moral standards. We would consider it brazenly immoral to tempt a reformed alcoholic by drinking in his presence or by daring a person we know to be reckless to do some impossible feat. Such behavior would increase their struggle, to be sure, but might well cause their utter downfall. A human being who acted in such a way would be called immoral; if God acts that way, why should we call his behavior the result of higher morality? (iii) God could mitigate a particularly terrible result in a stop-gap fashion by a miraculous intervention. It is not sufficient for the theist to reply that it is likely God *does* interfere often without our knowing it to prevent terrible consequences. This reply only terrifies one by suggesting how bad the universe might have been, but helps in no way to explain why it is not better than it is. (iv) It is logically possible on this view that men having free will should always choose to do wrong, and that even so, a universe of thoroughly evil men with free will would be intrinsically better than one of happy productive robots. The absurdity of this consequence suggests the falsity of the premises.

This last criticism has led to a reformulation of the free-will solution.[34] Not only is free will intrinsically good, this argument states, but it is also instrumentally good. It in fact produces more good consequences than evil ones. Moreover, it leads to beatitude achieved by man's own efforts and to the virtues achieved through suffering. This new version, however, is not much help. The claim is made that more often than not, free will results in desirable consequences rather than undesirable ones. But this claim is an empirical one of quantity (the question of what is desirable and undesirable is assumed to be the same for both theist and nontheist), and it is difficult indeed to see how anyone could have adequate evidence to establish its truth. It might possibly be the case, but we do not know that it is. Hence it might be a possible justification for God's granting free will, but we do not know that it is. Even worse, the fact that good outweighed evil in our universe, even if established, would not explain the willy-nilly distribution of good and evil. The claim that free will makes possible the achievement of beatitude and moral virtues through effort and suffering leads to difficulties already discussed in the first version of the free-will solution. Consummate bliss in loving God without suffering is not a self-contradictory concept. And the virtues nurtured through great suffering, as we have seen, are the very ones we try to avoid by removing the evil conditions of the world which make them necessary.

There is still a third version of the free-will solution favored by some contemporary philosophers who still depend upon Descartes' stimulating discussion of the problem of evil. According to Descartes, God has granted men both the power of willing freely (choosing his own volitions) and the power of understanding, neither of which is defective in itself. The trouble arises

> from the fact that the will is much more ample and far-reaching than the understanding, so that I do not restrain it within the same limits but extend it even to those things which I do not understand. Being by its nature indifferent about such matters, it very easily is turned aside from the true and the good and chooses the false and the evil. And thus it happens that I make mistakes and that I sin.[35]

But it need not be so. If I restrict my volition to what I know—that is, to what is clearly and distinctly reported by the understanding—then it cannot happen that I err. In so restricting myself, I use rightfully the freedom of will that God has given me.

Far from salvaging the free-will solution, Descartes' version encounters all the old difficulties and some new ones of its own. After all, God might have enhanced his gift to men by not only giving them free will but also a better understanding. Then man would have known better the right things to do and hence chosen to do them. Descartes, in fact, admits this point. He acknowledges that God could have given his understanding a clear and distinct comprehension of all the things about which he would ever deliberate. To explain why God does not increase or perfect man's understanding he suggests as a possibility "that the universe may be somehow more perfect because some of its parts are not free from defect while others are, than it would be if all parts were alike."[36] This view, of course, is nothing new. It amounts to the first version of the ultimate harmony view, or Augustine's aesthetic view of evil, and we have seen in detail the deficiencies in such maneuvers. Descartes exhibits the typical theistic effort to string together as many solutions to the problem of evil as possible, as if there were safety in numbers.

There are several objections that have often been advanced against all versions of the free-will solution which we have not used, and their absence may cause wonder among close students of the problem of evil. These objections have seemed important to some critics of theism; to us, however, it seems a mistake to use them. It is important to see why it is a mistake for anyone to use them. (i) The argument is sometimes used that God might have granted men free will and not only given them a disposition to act morally but have guaranteed their absolute goodness. The answer is that if God *guaranteed* the universal choice of right then men would be predestined to do right and hence would not really have free will. It is quite possible for God to guarantee that men should always do what is objectively right, but such a guarantee precludes the notion that men thereby exhibit moral virtue. To think that God could guarantee virtue is to confuse this logical impossibility with another claim that is logically possible but of no significance in the present context, namely, that God might have given men genuine free will and they might always choose to do the right thing.

(ii) Another argument against theism is that man's free will and God's omniscience (and omnipotence) are incompatible. Let X and Y represent two choices which are supposedly open to a person and P and Q respective consequences of each decision. If God is omniscient then he knows that the future holds, say, P and hence knows that the decision of the person must be X. Since there is no real alternative, the person does not have a free choice. Or if there are genuine alternatives then God cannot be all-knowing: The future is genuinely ambiguous. Calvinists have traditionally insisted on the omniscience of God and rejected the free-will solution to the problem of evil. Quasi-theists, on the other hand, keep free will as a solution but modify the traditional omni-characteristics of God. Writers in both of these camps pass too quickly over the Augustinian tradition which attempts to keep both the solution and the traditional view of God. According to contemporary Augustinians, in genuine cases of free choice nothing external to man's own deliberations, whether the origin be God, heredity, or environment, causes the decision to do X; God simply knows what the outcome of the deliberation will be. In knowing the outcome God does not bring it about. And the fact that the outcome is known does not entail that the person could not have chosen otherwise but only that he would not.

There is, to be sure, one sense in which the Christian concept of God and man's freedom would be clearly incompatible.[37] The Christian notion of Creator usually includes the view that God's will continues as a *sustaining cause* of every event, including men's decisions; hence if freedom of will means uncaused decision, it is incompatible with man's freedom. The Augustinian, however, only has to insist that he does not mean by freedom of will an uncaused decision but some notion of deliberation which is compatible with the concept of God as sustaining cause. This is difficult, admittedly, so the Augustinian might be forced to reject the notion of God's will as sustaining cause of all events. But is it legitimate to do this? And so the arguments and counter-arguments continue.[38]

We hope by now to have shown that the whole question of whether man's free will and the Christian concept of God are compatible notions is an extremely complicated issue, but the point is that while the outcome of the argument is crucial to Calvinists, Augustinians, and quasi-theists it is not in the least crucial to us. Even if it could be shown that the two notions are incompatible, this fact would be compatible with either the Calvinistic or quasi-theistic alternatives and so would not constitute a good reason for rejecting theism in favor of no belief at all. We have thus urged criticisms of the free-will solution which suggest that any religious cosmology that depends upon it is vulnerable. Hence the arguments we advance against traditional theism also apply to the quasi-theists who depend heavily on the concept of freedom in their theodicies.

NOTES

1. Antony Flew: *God and Philosophy*, p. 141.
2. H. J. McCloskey: "God and evil," *The Philosophical Quarterly*, X:102, 1960.

3. Michael Scriven: *Primary Philosophy*. New York, McGraw-Hill, 1966, p. 163.
4. *Ibid.*, p. 163.
5. F. R. Tennant: *Philosophical Theology*. Cambridge, U. P., 1930, vol. II, pp. 199-202.
6. C. S. Lewis: *The Problem of Pain*. New York, Macmillan, 1961, pp. 117-131. Austin Farrer: *Love Almighty and Ills Unlimited*. New York, Doubleday, 1961, pp. 71-94.
7. Lewis, *op. cit.*, p. 123.
8. One must avoid the erroneous assumption that God was forced either to make evolutionary laws exactly as they are or to abandon evolution altogether and create a world of static perfection.
9. Farrer, *op. cit.*, p. 79.
10. Wilmon H. Sheldon, passage from *God and Polarity*, reprinted in Daniel J. Bronstein, *et al.* (Eds.): *Basic Problems of Philosophy*. Englewood Cliffs, Prentice-Hall, Third Edition, 1964, p. 513.
11. McCloskey, *op. cit.*, p. 103.
12. *Ibid.*, p. 103.
13. Curt John Ducasse: *A Philosophical Scrutiny of Religion*. New York, Ronald Press, 1953, p. 361.
14. Nels F. S. Ferré: *Reason in Religion*. London, Nelson, 1963, p. 267.
15. There is something especially poignant about a small child's comments on the problem of evil. Robert Coles, a psychiatrist, recently made a study of the drawings of Negro children in the South. He was particularly interested in how they represented their skin color. One little Negro girl in Mississippi said after she had drawn a picture of herself: " 'That's me, and the Lord made me, but I must always remember that He did it, and it's His idea. So when I draw the Lord, He'll be a real big man. He has to be to explain about the way things are.' " [Robert Coles, "When I Draw the Lord He'll be a Real Big Man," *The Atlantic Monthly*, 1966, vol. 217, No. 5, p. 75].
16. John Stuart Mill, selection from *An Examination of Sir William Hamilton's Philosophy* included as an appendix in *Theism*, edited by Richard Taylor, New York, The Liberal Arts Press, 1957, pp. 89-96.
17. Cf. Chauncey Wright, *Philosophical Discussions*, edited by C. E. Norton, New York, Henry Holt and Co., 1877, pp. 358-59.
18. Augustine: *Works*, IX, Edinburgh, T. and T. Clark, 1873, pp. 181-82.
19. Farrer, *op cit.*, pp. 30-31.
20. *Ibid.*, pp. 23-31.
21. *Ibid.*, p. 61.
22. *Ibid.*, p. 65.
23. John Hick (Ed.): *Classical and Contemporary Readings in the Philosophy of Religion*. Englewood Cliffs, Prentice-Hall, 1964, p. 478.
24. Cf. Alfred Noyes, *The Unknown God*, New York, Sheed and Ward,

1940, pp. 274-75.

25. McCloskey, *op. cit.*, p. 108.

26. The doctrine of The Fall is usually associated with this view. Discussions of this explanation constitute an immense literature which dwarfs the output of philosophers of religion. The literary significance of the doctrine of The Fall would be difficult to overestimate. Milton's *Paradise Lost* is only one of the many literary masterpieces based on the doctrine. And the doctrine's influence on more or less popular religious belief outside belles lettres has been even greater. Its significance for systematic theology and philosophy of religion, however, is another matter. For a long time most philosophical theologians have regarded the doctrine as an embarrassment. But, at the risk of being accused of flogging a dead horse, we will briefly point out the deficiencies of the doctrine as a solution to the problem of evil. This can be conveniently done by simply summarizing what a theist has found inadequate about this solution.

   (1) The conditions which cause suffering (e.g. earthquakes) existed before the emergence of man and the possibility of sin.

   (2) The policy of punishing all for the sins of the first pair hardly accords with the best moral standards.

   (3) "It is impossible to conceive of wholly good beings in a wholly good world becoming sinful. To say that they do is to postulate the self-creation of evil *ex nihilo!* . . . The very fact that the creature sins refutes the suggestion that until that moment he was a finitely perfect being." [John Hick, *Evil and the God of Love*, New York, Harper and Row, 1966, pp. 285-86.]

27. George Arthur Buttrick: *God, Pain and Evil*. Nashville, Abingdon Press, 1966, p. 126.

28. *Ibid.*, p. 122.

29. *Ibid.*, p. 126.

30. *Ibid.*, p. 154.

31. H. H. Farmer: *The World and God*. New York, Harper and Brothers, 1935, p. 243.

32. The Thomists also offer a free-will solution to the problem of moral evil but with interesting variations that deserve separate notice. Maritain says that "we must hold with Saint Thomas that every creature is naturally fallible; God can no more make a creature, angel, or man, *naturally impeccable* than He can make a square circle." [Jacques Maritain, *God and the Permission of Evil*, Milwaukee, Bruce Pub. Co., 1966, p. 37. See also his earlier piece, *Saint Thomas and the Problem of Evil*, Milwaukee, Marquette University Press, 1942.] This is, of course, an argument used by many non-Thomistic theists. The Thomists, however, refine the free-will solution by the use of the Augustinian theory of evil as privation. They wish to describe God as responsible for good human acts but not for morally evil acts. The

cause of a morally evil act must, they suppose, be explained as non-being. If the cause were a positive being, God, as omnipotent and all-creative, would have had, in turn, to cause it and he would thereby lose his moral perfection.

This interesting combination of doctrines has the following difficulties.

a) All the criticisms we make in this section of the other versions of the free-will solution apply equally well to the Thomist version.

b) The Thomistic account of moral evil as the result of a "non-act" will not solve the problem of moral evil unless it can be shown that *only one kind* of human freedom is possible. However, as we indicate in this section and again in our discussion of John Hick, there is no impossibility in God's creating genuinely free human beings *with a different set of dispositions.* The Thomists, like many theists, assume that God must either create free human beings with exactly the dispositions they have now or create robots. This assumption is curiously similar to an assumption that a parent might make in defending his upbringing of a delinquent child. He might argue that he had only two choices: to respect the child's freedom, or to raise a puppet. Since those were the only possibilities, he cannot, he concludes, be blamed for his child's delinquency. Everyone recognizes that there are many different ways of respecting a child's dignity and some are much less apt to lead to delinquency than others. It is equally clear that there are different ways for God to create free human beings. No one is asking God to create *infallible* beings, just as no one is asking parents to raise infallible children. We are insisting merely that an omnipotent, all-good God could easily have created free creatures with *less* tendency to do moral evil. We need not here go into the metaphysics of the notion of "the free initiative of a non-act, of a nihilating, of a *not* to consider the rule." [*God and the Permission of Evil*, p. 38.] The concept of freedom is a notoriously complicated philosophical problem in its own right. One can accept without reservation the metaphysical account of moral evil as the result of a non-act and still ask the crucial question of why God did not create human beings with less disposition toward morally evil non-acts.

c) The criticisms we have given of the privation doctrine in connection with physical evil will apply to its use by the Thomists in the problem of moral evil.

d) The privation doctrine involves a further difficulty we have not mentioned previously. The doctrine is self-defeating. This fault is especially clear in the Thomist discussions. Journet quotes St. Thomas: "'Evil is not a part of the universe: it has neither reason nor substance nor accident, but only privation'" [Charles Journet, *The Meaning of Evil*, New York, P. J. Kenedy, 1963, p. 78]. Yet a few pages later he also quotes St. Thomas that "'if all evils were prevented, many good things would disappear from the universe. The life of the lion would not be preserved by the death of other animals.' " [*Ibid.*, p. 82.] If evil has no substance and is a mere privation, how can we suppose that it so often *causes* greater good in the long run. The doctrine of privation proves too much. If it is consistently held, no evil can be thought of as instrumentally good since obviously nonbeing cannot be an instrument. All the examples of ultimate harmony so dear to the theists must be discarded. Evil, according to the privation doctrine, can have no efficacy. Evil may have disappeared from the face of the earth, but it took with it an enormous amount of good.

33. McCloskey, *op. cit.*, p. 113.
34. *Ibid.*, p. 112.
35. René Descartes: *Meditations*, tr. L. J. Lafleur, New York, Liberal Arts Press, 1951, pp. 51-52. Quoted in Ducasse, *op. cit*
36. Descartes, *op. cit.*, p. 55.
37. Antony Flew, *op. cit.*, pp. 43-48.
38. See, e.g., Antony Flew: "Divine Omnipotence and Human Freedom," in *New Essays in Philosophical Theology*, edited by Flew and A. MacIntyre, London, SCM Press Ltd., 1955, pp. 144-169; Alvin Plantinga, "The Free Will Defence" in *Philosophy in America*, edited by Max Black, London, George Allen and Unwin, 1965, pp. 204-220; Nelson Pike, "Plantinga on the Free Will Defense: A Reply," *Journal of Philosophy*, LXIII:93-104, 1966; Plantinga, "Pike and Possible Persons," *Journal of Philosophy*, LXIII:104-108, 1966; Nelson Pike, "Divine Omniscience and Voluntary Action," *Philosophical Review*, LXXIV:27-46, 1965; John Turk Saunders, "Of God and Freedom," *Philosophical Review*, LXXV:219-225, 1966; Pike, "Of God and Freedom: A Rejoinder," *Philosophical Review*, LXXV:369-79, 1966; and Norman Kretzmann, "Omniscience and Immutability," *Journal of Philosophy*, LXIII:409-421, 1966.

Chapter Five

Theism II

T WO RECENT THEISTS whose work has been attracting considerable attention, and who, along with Farrer, are considered
among the subtlest contemporary defenders of theism, are John
Hick and Ian T. Ramsey. Not the least part of their work has
been directed to the problem of evil, and any consideration of
this problem which did not consider in some detail their work
would be woefully incomplete.

I

The intellectual honesty of John Hick is impressive. Unlike
the majority of Christian apologists he does not try to find safety
in the number of solutions but instead searchingly criticizes and
disowns many of the favorite solutions.[1] He concludes, nevertheless, that apologetics reduced to fighting trim is all the more
effective. He believes that a sophisticated combination of the
character-building and free-will solutions will serve. They show
evil to serve God's purpose of "soul-making."

Earlier we pointed out the difficulties involved in the usual
formulations of the character-building and free-will solutions.
We shall consider here how successful Hick is in avoiding these
difficulties.

According to Hick,

> man, created as a personal being in the image of God, is only the
> raw material for a further and more difficult stage of God's creative
> work. This is the leading of men as relatively free and autonomous
> persons through their own dealings with life in the world in which
> he has placed them, towards that quality of personal existence that
> is the finite likeness of God.[2]

The basic trouble, he says, with antitheistic writers is that "they assume that the purpose of a loving God must be to create a hedonistic paradise."[3] He concedes that evil is not serving any, even remote, hedonistic end, but insists that it is serving the end of the development of moral personalities in loving relation to God. It is logically impossible to do this either by forcing them to love him or by forcing them always to act rightly. A creature *forced* to love would not be genuinely loving and a creature *forced* to do the right would not be a moral personality. Only through freedom, suffering, and initial remoteness from God ("epistemic distance") can the sort of person God is looking for come about.

Before we discuss in detail the difficulties involved in Hick's position we will briefly describe three informal fallacies Hick adroitly uses in his solution. They are all fallacies which have been used in one form or another throughout the history of Christian apologetics, and we have had occasion to mention them in our discussion of other writers in the previous chapter. However, it will be convenient in discussing Hick's skillful and elaborate use of them to describe and label clearly these arguments: "All or nothing," "It could be worse," and "slippery slope."

All or nothing. This is the claim that something is desirable because its complete loss would be far worse than the evil its presence now causes. The erroneous assumption is that we must have this thing either in its present form and amount or not at all. But it is often the case that only *some* amount of the thing in *some* form is necessary to the achievement of a desirable end.

It could be worse. This is the claim that something is not really bad because it will be followed by all manner of desirable things. The erroneous assumption here is that showing that having these later desirable things is a great boon also shows that the original evil is a necessary and not gratuitous one. Actually it only shows that the situation would be still worse if the desirable things did not follow. To show that it could be worse does not show that it could not be better.

Slippery slope. This is the claim that if God once started eliminating evils of this world he would have no place to stop short of a "perfect" world in which only robots and not men were possible. The erroneous assumption is that God would have no criterion to indicate where on the slippery slope to stop and no ability to implement it effectively. The same argument is used in human affairs and the answer is equally clear. "Once we venture, as we sometimes must, on a dangerous course which may lead to our salvation in a particular situation but which may also be the beginning of our path to perdition, the only answer we can give to the question 'Where will you stop?' is 'Wherever our intelligence tells us to stop!'"[4]

Hick's use of the free-will solution is an example of the "all or nothing" fallacy. He concedes that there is an appalling amount of moral evil in the world but insists that it would be logically impossible for God to achieve his purpose of soul-making by creating puppets who always acted rightly. This is a position we have criticized elsewhere and we must show here how the same criticism applies to Hick.

Hick says that the difficulty with criticisms of the free-will solution has been that they suppose God would have done better to create man as a "pet animal" in a cage, "as pleasant and healthful" as possible.[5] Undeniably critics of the free-will solution have often made this mistake, but it is a mistake easily avoided. We are prepared to grant that a better world would not have been created by making men as pet animals. However, the damaging question is whether God had only two alternatives: to create men with the unfortunate moral inclinations they have at present or to create men as pet animals. There are clearly other alternatives. There are, after all, many different ways for a parent to guide his child's moral growth while respecting his freedom.

Perhaps an analogy will be helpful. God, as Hick views him, might be described as headmaster of a vast progressive school where the absolute freedom of the students is sacred. He does not want to force any children to read textbooks because, he feels, that will only produce students who are more motivated by fear of punishment than by love of knowledge for its own sake. Every student must be left to educate himself as much as possible. However, it is quite unconvincing to argue that because rigid regulation has horrible consequences, almost no regulation is ideal—there are dangers in either extreme. And it is just as much of a mistake to argue that because the possibility of God's creation of men as pet animals is ghastly to contemplate, God's creation of men with the sort of freedom they have now is the best possible choice.

One of Hick's more unfortunate uses of the "all or nothing" argument appears in his justification of man's "initial epistemic distance" from God. He suggests that God has deliberately refrained from giving much knowledge of himself to men for fear that it would jeopardize the development of "authentic fiduciary attitudes" in men. God is fearful (in our analogy) that "spoon-feeding" his creatures will prevent them from developing genuine intellectual curiosity. Because he thinks that constant and thorough spoon-feeding will ruin their intellects, he advocates contact between schoolboy and teacher only once a year.

But we are being too kind in our analogy. God does not even think it wise to deliver a matriculation address to each student. Almost all students must be content with meager historical records of a matriculation address in the distant past and a hope of a commencement speech in the future. It is no wonder there have been student riots. The countless generations before Christ were especially destitute of faculty-student contact. And even now the vast amount of humanity in non-Christian parts of the world find it difficult to be admitted to the soul-making school at all.[6]

Sometimes Hick feels the weakness of the "all or nothing" argument and accordingly shifts to the "it could be worse" strategy. "Christian theodicy must point forward to that final blessedness, and claim that this infinite future good will render worth while all the pain and travail and wickedness that has occurred on the way to it."[7] To be sure, we should be grateful to God for not tormenting us for an eternity, but the question remains of why he is torturing us at all. However, this strategy is beside the point. Hick must still show us how all the suffering in this world is the most efficient way of achieving God's goal. Merely to assure the student who is threatening riot that in his old age he will somehow come to regard the indignities of his student days as rather unimportant is not to explain why those indignities must be visited upon him at all.

Although Hick does not himself feel confident that in the Kingdom of God all men will completely forget their earthly sufferings, he suggests that, if such a loss of memory were to occur, it would help solve the problem of evil.[8] However, we can concede complete heavenly amnesia and this concession does not move us any closer to a solution. If a man were to torture his wife, and afterwards somehow to remove completely the memory of the torture from her mind so that she returned to her earlier love of him, this would certainly be better than retaining the painful memory, but it still would not explain the necessity of torturing her in the first place.

Hick, however, candidly admits to a feeling that neither of the two strategies discussed above is completely effective in the last analysis and realizes that he must face "excessive or dysteleological suffering."[9] Consequently he moves on to the "slippery slope" argument.

> Unless God eliminated all evils whatsoever there would always be relatively outstanding ones of which it would be said that He should have secretly prevented them. If, for example, divine providence had eliminated Hitler in his infancy, we might now point instead to Mussolini. . . . There would be nowhere to stop, short of divinely arranged paradise in which human freedom would be narrowly circumscribed.[10]

He claims, in other words, that there would be no way of eliminating some evils without removing all of them with the effect of returning us to the "all or nothing" situation.

This argument fails because the erroneous assumption is made that in the process of removing evils God would not be able precisely to calculate the effect of each removal and stop at exactly the point at which soul making was most efficiently achieved. Presumably at that point men would still suffer and complain about their suffering, but it would be possible to offer them an explanation of the necessity of this amount of suffering as a means to the end of soul making. In the analogy we used earlier, no matter how much is done to increase faculty-student contact there will still be some student complaints, but presumably it is possible to reach a point at which such students can be shown how the present amount of faculty-student contact is precisely the right amount to maximize creative intellectual activity.

Hick even comes to admit that this third strategy is no more effective than the first two.[11] He appears to be like a man flourishing toy weapons before an assailant, knowing that in the last analysis they cannot be effective, but hoping that the assailant will be scared off before he comes close enough to see that they are not genuine weapons. In the last analysis he must appeal to mystery. "I do not now have an alternative theory to offer that would explain in any rational or ethical way why men suffer as they do. The only appeal left is to mystery."[12]

Hick's use of mystery is not the usual appeal to mystical experience or commitment so often made by theists. He suggests that mystery, too, contributes to soul-making. Here again he uses the "all or nothing" argument and asks us to imagine a world which contained no unjust, excessive, or apparently unnecessary misery, a world in which suffering could always be seen to be either punishment justly deserved or a part of moral training.

> In such a world human misery would not evoke deep personal sympathy or call forth organized relief and sacrificial help or service. For it is presupposed in these compassionate reactions both that the suffering is not deserved and that it is *bad* for the sufferer.[13]

There are at least three ways of criticizing this strategy:

(A) It is quite possible to feel intense compassion for someone even though his suffering is understood to be an unavoidable means to an end, desirable both to the sufferer and to oneself. A husband may feel convinced that his wife's labor pains are a necessary means to a highly desirable end and at the same time feel great compassion. One can even feel compassion for the pain suffered by a criminal being punished in a way that one thinks is deserved.

(B) Even if some undeserved and unnecessary suffering is necessary to make possible compassion, it is obvious that a minute percentage of the present unnecessary suffering would do the job adequately.

(C) One must remember that while unjust suffering may increase compassion, it also creates massive resentment. This resentment often causes individuals indiscriminately to lash out at the world. The benefits of compassion are probably more than offset by the damage done by resentment.

However, Hick thinks that there is still one last justification for unjust suffering. He asks us to consider what would happen if all unjust suffering were eliminated. In such a world reward would be the predictable result of virtue and punishment the predictable outcome of wickedness. But in such a world doing right simply for its own sake—what Kant called the good will— would be impossible "for whilst the possibility of the good will by no means precludes that right action shall in fact eventually lead to happiness, and wrong action to misery, it does preclude this happening so certainly, instantly, and manifestly that virtue cannot be separate in experience and thought from its reward, or vice from its punishment."[14]

This solution, itself a sign that the end is near at hand, can be rejected with confidence for the following reasons.

(A) This effort to solve the problem of evil does not do justice to the good sense God presumably would have were he to exist. God would certainly have sense enough to ad- minister rewards and punishments in view of *motives* and not simply in view of what an agent *does*. It would already be an unjust response if God rewarded an agent for doing what is objectively right on prudential grounds alone.

(B) This effort misfires psychologically as well as theo- logically. If God usually rewarded men when they sincerely performed an act solely because it was right, this could only have a beneficial effect on human morality. If a parent regu- larly rewards the child who performs a good act only because he thinks it right more than he rewards a child performing the same act only to curry favor with the parent, this can only tend to reinforce the tendency to act virtuously.

(C) Even if completely regular rewarding of right-behavior would tend to undermine the good will, there is still every reason to believe that an enormous amount of the present unjust punishment could be eliminated without jeopardizing the possibility of acting from a sense of duty. The "all-or-nothing" fallacy is omnipresent in theistic arguments and its presence here at the end, after it had been supposedly rejected, comes as no surprise.

II

Under the influence of recent philosophical thought there has been a surge of linguistic analysis in theological circles. There has been a concerted effort to find the special and unique ways in which theological phrases are used and to discover how they are anchored to the empirical situations of ordinary life. Of the many endeavors along these lines, that of Ian T. Ramsey is one of the most sophisticated and satisfactory. He develops themes along strictly Christian theistic lines and believes that within this framework he has an adequate way of meeting the problem of evil.

Early positivists, according to Ramsey, tried to show, via some verifiability criterion, that religious assertions are meaningless. Under various criticisms, however, the criteria were invariably widened until religious assertions were only denied cognitive or scientific status. But what theologian, who know what he was about, would want to deny that? The problem, then, becomes one of clarifying the logic of theological discourse and discovering the sort of meaning religious assertions in fact have. The legitimacy of this endeavor was reinforced by those linguistic analysts who either implicitly or explicitly equate the meaning of a phrase with its use (as distinct from usage) and by those who stress the importance of performative utterances. The result has been that surge of "linguistic theology" wherein theological phrases are "anchored" in the empirical world without having their meaning exhausted by such empirical reference. There always remains a dimension of commitment and worship in all theological phrases which gathers up while it yet transcends its empirical elements.

Theological phrases are anchored in the empirical world, according to Ramsey, by using words in their ordinary ways as "models" and then appropriately qualifying them in a specially religious way. And since the Christian believes that God can be seen in all the words of his creation, he believes that any word can be so developed and used religiously. For the Christian theist God becomes the key word, "the irreducible posit," which presides over all language and toward which all qualified models lead. Such qualified models are the "currency" for expressing that special discernment which is uniquely Christian and that complete commitment which, of necessity, accompanies the discernment. And these qualified models are the means for evoking discernment and commitment on the part of nonbelievers. The Christian keeps using different sorts of qualified models until he hits upon the right one that "breaks the ice" or makes "the light dawn" for just this particular person.

The use of First Cause, Ramsey believes, is a good example of what he means by a qualified model. *Cause* provides the model from ordinary language and *first* modifies or qualifies it in the appropriately religious way. To begin with, *cause* specifies a development either forward or backward in time. We can think, for example, of a tree growing from an acorn or, over eons of time, being compressed into coal. The word first operates as a qualifier in the sense that it directs attention always backward until the "light dawns, the penny drops, the ice breaks" and we see that there must be something that completes the series and is logically prior to any series of causal stories, and hence that this first cause belongs to a logically different species than ordinary causes. *First Cause* unites and presides over all causal stories; it completes the sequence of causal stories by transforming it into something different. The series of proximate and remote causal explanations is transformed into a kind of motive-model explanation. A First-Cause explanation is quite like "because he decided to" and quite unlike "because he is an exhibitionist" in answer to the question, "Why did John dive from the high board?" Despite *grammatical* similarities, then, *First Cause* is not at all *logically* parallel to either *proximate cause* or *remote cause*. Naturalists have been misled by these grammatical similarities when they have argued in the following way. The very concept of self-cause, it has been argued, is a meaningless one because *cause* implies *predecessor* while *First Cause* both implies and denies *predecessor*. The naturalist who argues in this way is mistaken, and the explanation of his mistake is that he has confused two logically distinct forms of discourse.

Infinitely good, like most other theological phrases, can be explicated along similar lines. *Good* provides the model and *infinitely* the qualifier. This phrase is anchored in ordinary experience when we say that P is fairly good, Q is good, R is very good, S is intensely good . . . and God is infinitely good. But the latter is not simply the completion of the series. "In tracing such a sequence there is no intention of arriving at *God* as a last term; the intention is to continue long enough with the sequence to evoke a situation characteristically different from the terms which preceded it; until we have evoked a situation not just characterized by a goodness which we admire or feel stirred to follow, but a situation in relation to which we are prepared to yield everything, 'soul, life and all'."[15] *Infinite* qualifies *good* in a way that puts the latter outside of God language altogether. God is not simply good, one might say, but is good in a way beyond our ability to say—a discernment which indeed deserves total commitment. This qualified model again shows how the naturalist goes wrong when he argues in the following way. The very concept of infinitely good, he has said, is a meaningless one because *good* implies *better* while *infinitely good* entails both *better* and *good beyond which there is no better*. By qualifying the model *good* with *infinitely,* the naturalist continues, the word has been drained of all the meaning it ever had and the result is an empirical void. This argument, Ramsey says, blunders in the logical placing of God talk, failing, as it does, to take account of the special religious way that models are qualified.

The problem of evil arises for Ramsey in this qualified-model context in an interesting way. The Christian claim is that God can be seen in all the words of his creation and hence that all words suitably qualified can evoke a characteristically religious situation of discernment and commitment. But the word *evil* causes difficulty. *Infinitely evil* cannot characterize God as *infinitely good* can; rather it must refer to the Devil or some other principle of evil. But then there are two key words, God and Devil, and this will not do for theism. The problem of evil is to avoid this dualism of key concepts and the only way to do this is to show that talk about evil is consistent with the key concept of an infinitely powerful and good God.

Consistency may be achieved, Ramsey thinks, by different sorts of language models. For example, a train master might *permit* an engineer to make a mistake in order to learn an important lessen without *willing* his mistake. The same is true of God: Even though he wills good he sometimes permits evil to occur in order to create a harmonious community of free human beings who have learned responsibility, self-reliance, and so on. Thus we have a "language map" by which dualism is avoided. And yet the map is only a model and must be qualified, as always, with a word like eternal—God is eternally purposive and always draws good from evil.

Another model for avoiding dualism and showing the consistency of talk about God and evil is the use of *love*. Because they love their children and students, parents and schoolmasters develop general rules and regulations which are extremely beneficial overall even though in specific cases they produce undesirable hardships. For the same reason they allow children and students a certain amount of freedom of choice in order to develop responsibility even though upon occasion it is misused or even abused. God exhibits such love also in forming a universe with laws and regulations that produce beneficial results overall even though upon occasion they produce disasters. And he exhibits the same love in allowing men a certain amount of free will both because it is intrinsically valuable and because it is necessary for nurturing a sense of responsibility and self-reliance. Again, however, the model of *love* must be appropriately qualified when speaking of God by such words as supreme and infinite.

There are many other models which would develop the consistency of God and evil talk, but they all follow the same pattern as the ones described. There are, however, several important implications of all consistency language which can be ignored only at great risk of confusion. None of the model expressions, even when appropriately qualified, straightforwardly describes God. Rather expressions like "God exhibits eternal purpose," "God is supreme love," and so on tell us how we must talk about God if we wish honestly to face the evil in the world and at the same time square it with talk about God as infinitely powerful and good. The qualified models produce "consistency language" by which unwanted dualism can be avoided. Also, it is plain "that such a solution to the problem of evil as we have outlined brings with it as a *logical necessity* a total commitment to the universe." If we speak of God by using qualified models like supreme redeeming love, then "there must go with that the response of 'soul, life, and all.' Thus, properly speaking, the problem of evil is only 'solved' when we have not only formulated a consistent way of talking, but when that way of talking brings with it a commitment to the Universe which, as part of itself and in particular, struggles with and overcomes the evil from which the problem began."[16]

It is clear at once that while Ramsey's linguistic analysis is very useful in explicating the meaning of religious phrases it yields no solution or new insight into the problem of evil, based as it is on combinations and variations of traditional solutions.

In the first place, there are many ways in which we agree with his analysis and find it clarifying. We agree that religious assertions are meaningful in some sense; indeed we insisted upon this point ourselves in Chapter Three against those theists who tried to show the problem of evil to be meaningless. We also agree that religious phrases have a logical form different from straightforwardly empirical ones and yet are related to them also. The use of qualified models, analogies, or metaphors is standard practice in metaphysics, and there is little point in condemning or applauding such techniques wholesale. Sometimes they are meaningful and useful, other times not. Ramsey likewise, as we shall see, sometimes uses the techniques successfully, sometimes not.

Ramsey's use of the technique in the case of First Cause is not very successful. First, throughout this discussion, as everywhere in his work, there is a subtle ambiguity. The ambiguity consists in shifting back and forth implicitly from questions of meaning to questions of truth. The point of his discussion of First Cause presumably is to show that this notion makes sense and is not the semantical freak that naturalists say it is. Certainly Ramsey never tries to show that the First Cause argument *proves* that God exists. His Christian belief is not gained through any argument at all but is a matter of "discernment" and self-involvement. And yet, on the other hand, the qualified model of First Cause, like all qualified models, supposedly leads to that discernment which is the real ground of belief and commitment. So there is a truth claim, after all, embedded in all this analysis. But in the present case, as in many others, the truth claim makes no sense. No analysis of First Cause is going to produce that uniquely Christian discernment and commitment which is central and essential to everything that Ramsey believes and claims. The real discernment and commitment, it is clear, has nothing to do with language at all but is existential and historical in character. The most that analysis of concepts like First Cause can do is show that they are *compatible* with the Christian commitment even though they are useless in establishing it.

Second, and even more serious, Ramsey frequently fails with his language analysis in removing the stumbling blocks of meaninglessness and inconsistency in the path of theistic belief. The naturalist does think that the concept of First Cause is inconsistent and nothing Ramsey says successfully discounts it. The appearance of his success follows only from an inadequate presentation of the naturalist's criticism. The naturalist maintains only as a first move that *First Cause* both implies and denies *predecessor*. He is perfectly aware that if there were a First Cause it would have a nature different from that of efficient causes. Its *modus operandi* would indeed resemble ordinary motive models of action and not efficient cause models of movement. But the next move for the naturalist is this: Ordinary motive models of action, while they are autonomous and not to be "reduced" to efficient causes, always have necessary antecedents. Hence the naturalist believes that it is incumbent upon the theologian to show how *First Cause* not only exemplifies the motive model but also differs from ordinary motive models in having no antecedents at all. Theologians have responded with the concept of Self Cause, which incorporates both the notion that First Cause is a motive model and that it has no antecedent except itself. God both exists and is his own ground for existing. He is a Necessary Being, and so on. To the naturalist, however, this claim seems either like the old inconsistency in new guise or else a consistent but untenable metaphysics. In any case, the problems of First Cause need to be pursued far beyond the limit set by Ramsey. Whatever else he may be doing the naturalist is not simply making the mistake of projecting semantical similarity into logical similarity. The concept of First Cause, for anything Ramsey has shown to the contrary, still remains inconsistent and hence a stumbling block in the path of theistic belief.

Ramsey's discussion of *infinitely good* seems to us to be more successful, although not without difficulties of its own. The ordinary model of *good* presumably gives some understandable content to the claim that God is infinitely good. But God's goodness, Ramsey says, as always, is not the last term of the series. The model must be qualified. We must continue in the sequence, we are told, until we have evoked a situation not just characterized by a goodness which we admire or feel stirred to follow, but one in which we are prepared to yield everything— our soul, life, and all. This qualification of the model *good*, however, is weak and needs reinforcement. Running through a series does not help evoke the religious response of yielding all, since the leap from the best we know to God's goodness is not itself part of the series. What we need to see is not only how God's goodness is like ordinary goodness but how it differs from it. The proper qualification is to say that God's goodness is the *very source of all goodness* and hence the worthy object of complete yielding. It is *this* discernment which is uniquely religious and is brought about by a real, positive qualification, unlike Ramsey's simple negative ones. It may seem strange that we should be interested in strengthening a theist's position instead of tearing it down. However, upon reflection, it turns out not to be strange at all. It should be clear that it is important to us that *God is infinitely good* should be clearly meaningful, for without it there would be no problem of evil! We do believe that, by and large, religious phrases have enough meaning to be sensible, even though there are given difficulties in specific cases. The real problem for theism is to match up God talk with talk about *prima facie* gratuitous evil.

Ramsey's effort to remove the inconsistency between *God* and *evil* by introducing various qualified models is even less successful than his previous ones. It comes as a disappointing surprise to discover that he has offered no new solution or new combination of solutions whatever for the problem of evil. Every qualified model he presents turns out to be a traditional solution minus its traditional name. The willing-permitting model turns out to be a combination of ultimate harmony, free-will, and character-building solutions. The model of redeeming love turns out to be a combination of the free-will, character-building, and beneficial-general-law solutions to the problem of evil. (He also mentions the Fall solution separately.) These traditional theistic solutions, separately and in various combinations, have all been found to have fatal difficulties. To establish this fact is the overall point of the previous chapters in this book. Ramsey not only does not adequately answer criticisms but does not even consider them, not even the most obvious ones. Until they are met, the consistency models offered by Ramsey do not even begin to do the job required of them. He has not shown in the slightest way that they remove the *prima facie* incompatibility between God and evil talk. We agree wholly with Ramsey that "God talk" makes some sort of complicated sense, at least sometimes, and that the qualified models he advances to solve the problem of evil make sense. They make good sense, but unfortunately for the theist they are unsuccessful. This inability to square talk about *God* and *evil* constitutes, as we have insisted throughout the book, the main reason for not accepting that framework of language in which Christian phrases admittedly make sense. There are, of course, considerations of an existential and historical sort which lead people to accept this language framework. But the inability to match talk about *prima facie* gratuitous evil with talk about a theistic God constitutes, in turn, a good reason for rejecting such a framework. Retrospectively the existential considerations become suspect if the language framework they qualify is unable to square the many diverse dimensions of human experience.

It is interesting to speculate why Ramsey is content not to meet the obvious difficulties of the solution which he offers to the problem of evil. The reason is perfectly clear and is not unfamiliar to us by now. Even if something is wrong with all theodicies, the theist argues, we are not defeated, only embarrassed. We know on existential, rational, and historical grounds that the Christian God exists and hence we know that there can be no gratuitous evil in the world even though we are unable to say how the gratuity is avoided. We have responded to this maneuver in a five-fold manner in Chapter One and will not repeat the performance in detail here. Suffice it to say here that this maneuver is essentially a version of the ultimate harmony solution and hence does not constitute an ultimate retreat for the theist after all. Besides, this maneuver has epistemic difficulties with the concept "to know." Theists say that they *know* that God exists in spite of their inability to account for gratuitous evil. However, as we have seen before, if the theist wants to say that he *knows* that God exists, he must not simply be certain of being right and happen in fact to be right, but he must have evidence adequate to warrant his degree of belief. And when he ignores the negative evidence of gratuitous evil, it is clear that he does not have adequate evidence to warrant his Christian confidence.

Much of Ramsey's work, and in particular his attitude toward evidence, hinges on his conception of the nature of metaphysics. In his use of "qualified models," Ramsey is just one of a host of Anglo-American metaphysicians who have recently made much use of metaphors, analogies, and models in metaphysics. This reference to models is part of a widespread effort to rebuild metaphysics in the wake of logical positivism. The well-known fact that models are a necessary part of scientific method lends empiricistic respectability to their use in metaphysics and theology. It has been repeatedly pointed out that metaphysicians cannot be accused of sinning against the canons of scientific method in their use of metaphors when the high priests of science (the theoretical physicists) are doing it themselves.

But Ramsey, like many other contemporary metaphysicians, realizes that it may be thought that models and metaphors in metaphysics and theology (indeed even in science) are merely heuristic devices or "jingles," and consequently he insists that they are not simply "link devices" between different contexts. They are fundamentally grounded in inspiration or disclosure, and "we can spend our lives elucidating ever more faithfully the mystery in which metaphors and models are born."[17] However, he cautions against putting too much stock in any one model. Instead we should rely on a "never-ending series of metaphorical inroads" because theology demands and thrives on a diversity of models.[18] All these models are to be judged on the basis of their "ability to point to mystery"[19] or to "articulate"[20] the insight or disclosure in which they were born.

Since the disclosure is said to have objective reference,[21] it might be supposed that one could deduce a verifiable event from the theological model in the same way that one can deduce verifiable effects from any meaningful scientific model; however, Ramsey emphatically denies that such verifiable deduction can be made from theological models though such models are just as meaningful as their scientific counterparts.[22] Instead, a theological model stands or falls "according to its success (or otherwise) in harmonizing whatever events are to hand." A theological model works more like the fitting of a shoe than the "yes" or "no" of a deductive roll call.

> In other words, we have a particular doctrine which, like a preferred and selected shoe, starts by appearing to meet our empirical needs. But on closer fitting to the phenomena the shoe may pinch. When tested against future slush and rain it may be proven to be not altogether watertight or it may be comfortable—yet it must not be too comfortable. In this way, the test of a shoe is measured by its ability to match a wide range of phenomena, by its overall success in meeting a variety of needs. Here is what I might call the method of empirical fit which is displayed by theological theorizing and it is a concept that I say a little more about in the next lecture.[23]

The ultimate mark of a model's success in this harmonizing is the total commitment it finally evokes.[24]

This is an interesting way of understanding the nature of metaphysical method. Indeed, there is much in Ramsey's discussion of metaphysics that we applaud. We wholeheartedly agree with Ramsey in his defense of the meaningfulness of metaphysics and, in particular, his defense of the legitimacy of the use of models in metaphysics.[25] The question, however, is not one of the legitimacy of metaphysics and its use of models but rather of the legitimacy of the particular metaphysical models Ramsey is recommending. We agree that *some* models can be used to construct satisfactory systems of metaphysics but at the same time insist that it is abundantly clear that any theistic model has grave deficiencies. Ramsey assumes throughout his discussion of models in metaphysics and theology that because some models are clearly successful, any model (e.g., the theistic model) has at least "tentative" success. This is a curious assumption. Every metaphysical model must be considered on its own explanatory merits and not merely accepted uncritically because it is as truly a model as any other. But in any case, whether or not they have tentative success, theistic models invariably fail in matching up the diverse elements of experience and hence fail the very test that Ramsey proposes for an adequate metaphysical model.

According to Ramsey, there is no particular theistic model used in speaking of God that is beyond criticism.[26] When criticisms of a model are made, he suggests that we must continue to qualify it with the hope of meeting all the criticisms. This critical attitude, however, is more apparent than real. An uncritical attitude quickly becomes evident in his notion of "the disclosure."

> . . . we are to be tentative, but always contextually tentative, about our theology, while grounding that theology in a disclosure of God.[27]
> . . . *models* of God can be and always are being *taken* away, criticized, graded, and ordered, and we are committed in this way to an endless explication of what cosmic disclosure reveals. We can be sure about God; but we must be tentative in theology.[28]

Ramsey makes it plain that this disclosure is what in philosophy has been traditionally called intuition.[29] We have, he thinks, an incorrigible intuition of God, and the problems of theology are merely those of trying to do justice to this intuition by the constant improvement of our theological language. What Ramsey somehow fails to see is that in describing his intuition as an intuition *of God* he has already introduced a model and therefore has begged the question.

Probably the easiest way to make clear Ramsey's mistake is to contrast his intuition or disclosure with Bradley's. Ramsey often refers approvingly to Bradley's metaphysical method. He explicitly likens his "disclosure" to Bradley's "immediate experience."[30] It is amazing that Ramsey in his enthusiasm for his disclosure forgets the well-known fact that Bradley emphatically denied that one's experience of the Absolute is experience of God.[31] The point is simply that different metaphysicians have different intuitions and many of them insist that their intuitions are not of a theistic reality. It will not do to treat one's metaphysical intuition as incorrigible when there are other metaphysicians with quite incompatible intuitions of their own which they regard as equally incorrigible. It also will not do to appeal to "total commitment" since materialists, for example, find themselves just as moved to total commitment by another "integrator word."[32]

However, we are not suggesting that intuition must be expunged from metaphysics any more than we are suggesting that it should be expunged from science. On the contrary, we hold with Russell that intuition or insight is often the source of true beliefs but not a sufficient guarantee of their truth.[33] Ramsey confuses intuition as a method of discovery with intuition as a method of verification. One can strongly recommend intuition for the former while condemning it for the latter. And one is forced to condemn it for the latter because there are so many competing intuitions; one must deal with those who have a metaphysical intuition of mechanical materialism and those who intuit a Manichean reality as well as those to whom a theistic reality is disclosed.

If one's disclosure is not incorrigible, what then are the legitimate grounds for judging a metaphysical model? Ramsey is quite right in saying that a metaphysical model is to be judged "by its ability to match a wide range of phenomena, by its overall success in meeting a variety of needs." And when one applies these criteria of judgment to the theistic model, it is plain that it is a failure. The burden of the whole analysis presented in this book is that the problem of evil reveals a wide range of events which cannot be matched with any theistic metaphysics no matter how far the words omnipotence, all-goodness, and evil are stretched. It will not do to reply that there are *prima facie* incompatibilities only between certain words in a particular theological language and that, with a little ingenuity, Ramsey can alter the language enough (i.e. add qualifiers) to remove these difficulties. We have not shown merely that *one* theological language contains these *prima facie* incompatibilities. We have analyzed an enormous variety of theological languages in the whole spectrum of theology and have found that they appear in every one. We are forced to conclude that there is a quite fundamental fault in the model regardless of the particular theological language in which it appears.

NOTES

1. John Hick: *Evil and the God of Love.* New York, Harper and Row, 1966, pp. 1-204.
2. *Ibid.,* p. 290.
3. *Ibid.,* p. 292.
4. Sidney Hook: *The Paradoxes of Freedom.* Berkeley, University of California Press, 1964, p. 48.
5. Hick, *op. cit.,* p. 293.
6. Some may protest that our use of a school analogy shows quite clearly that we have mistakenly understood Hick to be talking about moral rather than theological evil and about goodness rather than righteousness. However, this change in terminology will not affect the argument in the slightest. We are not assuming a utilitarian or any other theory of value; we are granting Hick any theory of value he likes. We may not ourselves be excited by the prospect of souls being made or by people becoming righteous, but we are granting this interest and then asking whether righteousness is being produced in a way that we would expect in a world presided over by an omnipotent, all-good God. We argue that it is not. It may be true that righteousness is being *less*

ineffectively produced than hedonistic values, but that hardly shows that the former is being produced in a way compatible with theism. It would be foolish for someone who has gone out of business to boast of his business success to another person who has gone out of business on the grounds that he did not go out of business so *soon.*

7. *Ibid.,* p. 376.
8. *Ibid.,* p. 386.
9. *Ibid.,* p. 363.
10. *Ibid.,* p. 363.
11. *Ibid.,* p. 369.
12. *Ibid.,* pp. 369-70.
13. *Ibid.,* p. 370.
14. *Ibid.,* p. 371.
15. Ian T. Ramsey: *Religious Language.* New York, The Macmillan Company, 1963, p. 77.
16. *Ibid.,* p. 99.
17. Ian T. Ramsey: *Models and Mystery.* London, Oxford U.P., 1964, p. 53.
18. *Ibid.,* p. 60.
19. *Ibid.,* p. 61.
20. *Ibid.,* p. 71.
21. *Religious Language,* p. 30.
22. Ian T. Ramsey: *Religion and Science.* London, SPCK, 1964, pp. 70-71.
23. *Models and Mystery,* p. 17.
24. *Religious Language,* p. 56.
25. See the opening section of Peter H. Hare, "Religion and Analytic Naturalism," *Pacific Philosophy Forum,* May 1967, for a defense of precisely this sort of metaphysics.
26. *Religious Language,* p. 89. Also Ian T. Ramsey, *On Being Sure in Religion,* London, The Athlone Press, 1963, p. 23.
27. *On Being Sure in Religion,* p. 90.
28. Ian T. Ramsey: *Christian Discourse.* London, Oxford U.P., 1965, p. 89.
29. Ian T. Ramsey (Ed.): *Prospect for Metaphysics.* London, George Allen and Unwin, 1961, pp. 175-76. Also *Religion and Science,* p. 6.
30. *Religious Language,* p. 59.
31. F. H. Bradley: *Appearance and Reality.* London, George Allen and Unwin, 1893, p. 447.
32. *Prospect for Metaphysics,* p. 163.
33. Bertrand Russell: *Selected Papers of Bertrand Russell.* New York, The Modern Library, 1927, p. 30.

Chapter Six

Quasi-Theism

I

ONE MAJOR STRATEGY is left and has been favored by those modern philosophers who have an interest in metaphysical speculation. This strategy is to combine the desirable characteristics of a theistic God with the desirable ones of a temporal or pantheistic God; thereby to produce a hybrid conception that both solves the problem of evil and is a fit object of worship. This is the interesting move we have been calling quasi-theism. The quasi-theists base both their criticism of theism and their own hybrid conceptions of God on elaborate metaphysics of a process and evolutionary sort. We shall examine these metaphysical commitments, some briefly and others in great detail, and show why they are incapable of doing the job expected of them.

In order to show how quasi-theists work we must first consider the traits of deity which a desirable hybrid must combine (and eliminate). Charles Hartshorne conveniently lists five traits: God must be Eternal, Temporal, Conscious, Knowing, and World Inclusive. God, that is, in some aspects of his reality must be devoid of change, in some aspects capable of change, be aware of self, omniscient, and have all things as constituents.[1] Each of these traits has its advantages and its disadvantages. The object of the quasi-theistic metaphysician in modifying the conception of God is somehow to combine all the advantages of these traits.

(A) *Eternal.* The advantages of a conception of God as eternal is that it suggests perfection, permanence, spirituality, omnipotence, and the ability to create and control the world.

104

This conception has a disadvantage in that it suggests a God that is remote, impersonal, and unsympathetic. Such a God seems to have the power to remove gratuitous evil though he does not do so.

(B) *Temporal.* This conception of course has the advantages missing in the previous conception. A conception of God as temporal suggests immanence and sympathy. Since he can change, he can be moved by human suffering and prayer. A temporal God also has the advantage in that it is presumably easier to get empirical evidence for his existence since he is not outside our world of change. Furthermore, such a conception of God solves the problem of evil (in a sense) by guaranteeing constant change toward the good even though (because he is not omnipotent) he cannot eliminate all gratuitous evil.

(C) *Conscious.* A conception of God as conscious has the advantage in that it suggests a personal being. It has the disadvantage of it being difficult to conceive of such an immense consciousness in naturalistic terms, and so the empirical evidence for his existence must be comparatively slight.

(D) *Knowing.* A conception of God as omniscient has the advantage in that it gives God the ability to predict the future, a means necessary to the control of the universe for the good. It also suggests a God who is in touch with all the desires and sufferings of creatures. It has the disadvantages that it is both in conflict with human freedom and makes God responsible for the evil he foresees.

(E) *World-Inclusive.* A conception of God as world-inclusive has the advantage in that it is easy to produce evidence for what is natural. It also has both the advantage of suggesting a God that is not remote and the advantage of giving men a feeling of importance because God needs them for his being. It has the disadvantage of suggesting a God who is not a being separate from the world, and thus not capable of personal relations with distinct beings in the world and not capable of guaranteeing the triumph of good from the outside. Moreover, such a God necessarily includes evil in his own being.

II

We can only suggest here the immense number of ways in which recent metaphysicians have tried to combine the advantages of the traits involved in these conceptions of God.

There are some who have put an extreme emphasis on the temporal while still making some effort to combine this with traits which are traditionally worshipped. Henri Bergson,[2] H. N. Wieman,[3] and a legion of other metaphysicians have identified God with emergent evolution and natural creativity in general without attributing consciousness (in the ordinary sense) to him. The variations on this theme are breathtaking. W. H. Sheldon finds deity in the operation of chance in evolution.[4] Louis Berman uses the notion of a psycho-continuum.[5] W. P. Montague has speculated brilliantly on the basis of the notion of potential energy.[6] Josiah Royce's teacher, Joseph LeConte, speaks of a "Divine Energy" and "an effluence from the Divine Person [which] flows downward into Nature to rise again by evolution to recognition of, and communion with, its own Source."[7] These philosophers are eloquent indeed in their descriptions of the deity. Bergson, for example, argues for mystical experience of the *élan vital*. Creativity obviously suggests to him, as it does to many other quasi-theists, a powerful, if unconscious, will.

This conception has the advantage of being a process whose reality cannot easily be denied. It also has the advantage that in his limited power and lack of consciousness he cannot be held responsible for evil, and it suggests a quasi-theistic movement toward the good. However, this is weak as a hybrid because it lacks the idea of a permanent, supreme, personal, conscious being who can perform such theistic functions as answering prayer, and also because it is difficult to consider such a God all-good since many of the products of creativity are evil.

Other philosophers, such as Samuel Alexander, have attempted to combine temporalism with permanence and consciousness by identifying God with the whole of space-time and its permanent *nisus* toward novelty in which the consciousness of God is constantly increasing.[8] But this also is weak as a hybrid because there is no idea of a permanent, *completed,* supreme personality. And even the already evolved mind of God is so tied to the processes of emergence that it seems hardly personal. The only way that such philosophers can, under these conditions, find genuine personal consciousness in God is to commit themselves to straightforward idealism in which all reality is construed as mental; such idealism forces them to sacrifice the traditional theistic emphasis on the contrast between the infinite divine mind and the natural world created by God. Moreover, God in this conception is not all-good as in traditional theism but is thought to be above good and evil.

The most appealing way to escape the failings of the temporalistic emphasis on evoultion is simply to identify God with reality as a whole in such a way that he is not simply a creative principle but is the remote and eternal *whole.* This pantheism has an advantage in that it conceives of God as infinite in all his traits as traditional theism does; but God then loses his status as a distinct being separate from the world and capable of creating and controlling it. Such a God also appears to be not all-good since the whole of reality contains evil.[9]

III

Brightman, Whitehead, Hartshorne, and Royce have all clearly recognized the grave dangers attendant upon all forms of quasi-theism and have made brilliant attempts to overcome them. Their influence is very great, and we will examine their work in detail. Brightman, Whitehead, and Hartshorne work toward a hybrid theism-temporalism, while Royce labors to unite aspects of theism and pantheism. Fascinating as their efforts are, they are no more successful, as we shall see, than the numerous other variations of quasi-theism.

IV

Brightman retains the theistic notions of a personal, conscious God who is worthy of worship and he retains the concept that good will prevail over evil in the long run in his notion of an evolutionary movement toward increased value. He also retains the essential Christian notions of atonement and redemption. However, the problem of evil convinced him that unlimited power of God, among other traditional theistic notions, must be abandoned.[10]

Brightman was a careful critic of all theodicies and, becoming convinced of their universal inadequacy, came to believe that some evil is genuinely gratuitous. He called such evils "dysteleological surds," by which he meant that they are evils which cannot be expressed in terms of any value just as surds in mathematics are quantities which cannot be expressed in rational numbers. He also believed that certain empirical facts conclusively suggest the existence of gratuitous evil. A real difficulty for religion "arises from the cruel and irrational waste and the seemingly aimless futility which evolutionary studies have revealed."[11] Moreover there appears to be pointless evil in the destructive forces of nature and in the agonies caused by disease.

Brightman's conviction that some evil is gratuitous led him to his theory of the Finite God. Such evil occurs in spite of God because there is something in his own nature which he cannot wholly control. According to Brightman, God's nature— as distinct from his will—has two distinct aspects: the eternal divine reason, and a passive element which enters into every one of his conscious states, as sensation and impulse enter into man's. It is this passive element in his own nature which contitutes a problem for God. He cannot always directly guide it to produce good results. Evil consequences sometimes occur, but they occur in spite of God's will and not as a result of it as the traditional theist maintains. In the long run, however, Brightman continues, God's will is triumphant. "He cannot allow any evil that will permanently frustrate his purpose. He may delay, but he cannot fail."[12] This point is important to Brightman for he repeats it in various contexts. "His will is adequate to extract value even from the most adverse possible circumstances."[13] "[God can] find a meaning in every situation, a good beyond every evil."[14] "God is . . . perfect in power to derive good from all situations, but not in power to determine in detail what these situations will be."[15]

In addition to denying God's unlimited power, Brightman also rejects other traditional theistic assumptions about God. Against the traditionalist he argues that the concepts of God's will and his nature must be kept distinct. Theists who follow Aristotle in saying that God is "self-caused" and "pure actuality" are mistaken. This view makes God pure self-caused will and leaves his nature without any content. But any being must be *something* and so have a nature: "a mere ghostly will would have nothing to operate on; it would be contentless and formless chaos."[16] That God has some nature independent of his will— what Brightman calls "the Given"—is necessary on metaphysical grounds; that part of his nature is passive and causes problems for God is required by the existence of gratuitous evil.

Brightman also rejects the traditional theistic view of creation *ex nihilo*. The Augustinian concept of God creating the world from nothing, he says, is neither scriptural nor reasonable. It does not accord with the account in *Genesis,* and it is unreasonable since it presupposes that God created time and existed before time as Pure Form without content. Brightman by contrast conceives of God as a divine craftsman who fashioned the world from a preexisting chaotic material. For him creation was not a single act in time by an omnipotent God, but is an eternal process in which God strives with chaos to bring into being beauty, order, and value.[17]

Brightman attacks the traditional eternalistic view of God and puts in its place his temporal view. He denies that God determines all events and then simply watches their predetermined unfolding. There is novelty in the world, both by God's own nature and by the freedom of finite beings; hence God must work in time and history shaping and molding the universe in accordance with changing conditions, always bringing out the greatest amount of value. Evolution, Brightman thought, presents evidence of God's creative power at work. The process is hampered by the passive aspects of God's nature—certainly a God of unlimited power would not have to bring about anything indirectly through evolutionary means—but the whole evolutionary process is clearly teleological in its drift. This temporal view of God provides man with a source of optimism, for God "has more to do than he has yet done."[18]

The psychological and moral appeal of a temporal God, Brightman concludes, is much greater than that of the traditional theistic God. It is more natural to pray to a finite God, he says, "who may be moved by our infirmities, than to an Absolute, whose decrees are eternally fixed."[19] Moreover, belief in a finite God provides moral incentives which are lacking when God is conceived to be infinite in power.

Brightman is quite successful in pointing out the weaknesses of traditional theism, but the alternative quasi-theism which he puts in its place is equally vulnerable. This is frequently the way with theological disputes. Each disputant is right in his negative claims and wrong in his positive ones. In trying to avoid the difficulties of theism, Brightman encounters new and related problems. And it is not wholly clear that he ever successfully resolves the difficulty of gratuitous evil. Moreover, his own concept of a finite God has just as many obscure and rationally defective aspects as traditional views. Brightman's quasi-theism falls heir to the following specific difficulties.

(A) Brightman has difficulty in justifying his belief that there is an evolutionary movement toward the good—his equivalent of the theistic view that good will prevail over evil in the long run. As long as God is conceived to be unlimited in power and goodness, there is no difficulty in maintaining that his very existence insures a preponderance of good or, in the long run, the substantial triumph of good. But when God is conceived to be limited in power in order to account for gratuitous evil, there is no longer any assurance that God is sufficiently unlimited to bring about this desirable denouement. Brightman apparently thought that just as empirical evidence of cruelty and waste in the evolutionary process shows that God is limited, so empirical evidence of design and progress inherent in the evolutionary process shows that God has the upper hand in the universe. But putting the question on an empirical basis has grave disadvantages. To an impartial observer, the battle between good and evil seems like a fluctuating affair. And even if the drift is toward the success of good now, what will the long run show? Perhaps the will of God and the rational aspect of his nature are rallying now but will eventually be overcome by the passive aspect of his nature. The empirical evidence is compatible with either interpretation. Hence theists have wisely built in the notion that good will prevail at the very beginning in the form of God's nature.

Brightman encounters other difficulties in his efforts to show that a finite God can assure the triumph of good. For him there can be no really ultimate triumph of good. Evil is never defeated permanently. The battle against the passive elements in God's nature continues eternally. To be sure, according to Brightman, the generation of good from the difficulties caused by the Given continues ever onward and upward throughout eternity, but by the same token evil elements are eternally active and are never ultimately subdued and removed.

Moreover, if God really has sufficient power to insure the relative triumph of good throughout eternity, then one wonders why he does not eliminate along the way many evils when such a removal would seem to require far less power than such *guaranteed* success in the long run. What Brightman says is equivalent to a United States Senator saying that, although it may take a long time, he can absolutely guarantee that eventually he will persuade President Johnson to stop the war in Vietnam, but in the meantime there is nothing that he can do to stop a single napalm bombing. Such a claim at best would not be very reassuring.

(B) Brightman, unlike the traditional theist, has a serious problem of explaining why God created any world at all out of the original formless matter. The theist with good conscience can say that God created the world because it would be intrinsically good to do so and because he would be able essentially to control the nature and amount of evil. But Brightman admits that God cannot prevent the occurrence of gratuitous evil; hence he has to explain why, under such conditions, he chose to create a world at all. Even if there is more good than evil in the world this fact would not touch the injustice of gratuitous evil. To say that a finite God may justly create a world with gratuitous evil, since God assumes the responsibility of redemptive love, does not constitute an adequate reply. The notion of redemption is ambiguous here. It cannot mean the redemption of sin and the subsequent evils thereof, because moral evil is not what Brightman is trying to account for in his concept of the Given. If redemption is thought of as divine insurance that the pains of this life will be more than compensated for in another, one wonders how a finite God has the power to insure such compensation. If he has such tremendous power over the Given, why is he not using it to eliminate many of the more easily eliminated evils of the world *in the first place?* If he has such power, that is just another reason to believe that the evils are indeed gratuitous.

(C) Brightman's concept of the passive nature of God is ambiguous. It has two possible interpretations, and only two, and each one leads to equally disastrous results. How does God's will work with and control the passive element of the Given? In many places Brightman clearly states that the will of God through its own force imposes good results on what is basically opposed to goodness. In this case the passive part of God's nature is positively evil, that is, evil by its own nature, and God then can no longer be considered unlimited in goodness. He becomes a strange dualistic god who possesses in his own being the incompatible nature of a god of light and a god of darkness—a concept which Brightman must avoid at all costs.

On the other hand, Brightman in many places clearly states that the will of God gradually draws good from the passive part of the Given through careful manipulation, in which case the Given is not something evil in nature which must be overcome by force but simply has conflicting elements from which God's will eventually draws the maximum amount of good possible. On this view, evil is nothing positive in its own right but is simply the privation of good. This answer saves God's unlimited goodness, to be sure, but amounts essentially to the Augustinian view of evil and hence does not require Brightman's concept of a finite god. God simply produces the best possible results from a basically good system which has necessarily conflicting elements. Why does this compromise God's unlimited power?

(D) The fact that physical laws have been to all intents and purposes the same for eons of time poses a problem for Brightman which the theist does not have. The theist assumes that God with his infinite foreknowledge calculated in advance exactly what physical laws would create the most possible good. However, the believer in a finite God cannot take this position. Because he must work the best he can with resistant material and must ask the cooperation of free agents, a finite God is never in a position to predict with accuracy what action in the future is going to be in the best interests of the cosmos. Surely one would expect an all-good God working under these conditions to be much more flexible in imposing physical laws on the cosmos than appears to be the case. Although, of course, one would not suppose it in the best interests of the cosmos for God to overturn the laws constantly, nevertheless one would expect him to be much more flexible than he apparently is if he were really interested in the best for the world. The apparent fixity of law seems to favor the traditional view of God rather than Brightman's—if one is going to believe in God at all.

(E) The poor communication between God and man also poses a problem for Brightman which the theist does not have. A theist does not have to worry about the fact that God has not made his existence and purposes plain to the vast majority of mankind. Since an all-powerful God is able to insure the triumph of good single-handedly without soliciting the cooperation of men, he does not need to inform men of his policies unmistakably. But once one conceives of God as limited in power and as requiring the cooperation of men, then God, if he is to do his job with any effectiveness, must inform all men of his intentions. Yet it is obvious that the vast majority of men are unsure of the purposes of such a god, not to speak of their uncertainty as to his very existence.

Consider an analogy. A group of junior executives in a branch office of a far-flung business empire are discussing rumors that there is a "big boss" in the New York office who is responsible for the creation and continuing success of the business. One man says that he has met an employee who has actually seen this executive, but others are skeptical and suggest that the business was created and has grown as a result of the efforts of a very large number of individuals. The men also discuss rumors about what the overall policy of the company is. There is a great deal of disagreement; the majority seem very unsure what the policy is, if there is one at all. An executive from a rival organization happens along and is amused by their speculation. He remarks that any top executive of a business empire who fails to inform unmistakably all his employees of his existence and of his policies is either a fool or a knave. How can this executive expect to get intelligent, effective cooperation from his subordinates if he does not even convince them of his existence and tell them clearly about his policies? Either the executive is so foolish that he does not realize that cooperation requires communication or else he is so sinister that he enjoys making his creatures live in a world of ambiguous appearances.

(F) Finally, the "moral" argument advanced by Brightman turns out to be useless. According to this argument, the theist is committed to the view that all evil somehow serves a good end, a view which is, however, intolerable to man's religious and moral consciousness. It destroys the very distinction between good and evil, since everything we ordinarily call evil is "really" or "ultimately" good. Such a view undermines moral incentive, since, on this view, whatever is, is right. The concept of a finite God, on the other hand, gives moral endeavor real significance; man joins with God in the eternal advance against evil.

No doubt the negative part of this argument, directed against the theist, is a telling one. But the point about moral endeavor has no independent force in favor of a limited God, since the naturalistic alternative makes equal sense out of moral endeavor. If there is no God at all, then even more forcefully "whatever is, is right" is mistaken, and moral endeavor becomes wholly necessary if there is to be any justice at all in the world.

V

Whitehead and Hartshorne retain the theistic notions of a God separate from creation who is worthy of worship and they also retain the concept that good will prevail in the equivalent concept of an evolutionary increase in the achievement of value.[20] However, as a result of their process metaphysics and the problem of evil, they reject the unlimited power of God among the traditional theistic notions, although they do not talk about a finite God in the straightforward way that Brightman does.

Whitehead modifies the traditional notion of the unlimited power of God in several ways. The power of God is "relative," he thinks, because God cannot annul the past and cannot deny freedom to actual occasions.[21] Since actual occasions have freedom, some evil is the inevitable result. Moreover, he is not the creator of the physical world in the usual theistic sense. God's creative power, rather, consists in his divine evocation of novelty from actual occasions.

The use of the word relative rather than limited is crucial. Whitehead and Hartshorne do not believe that God's power is limited by natural events which thwart his will but say that his power is relative to actual occasions in the sense that they provide the conditions for the exercise of his creative power. God remains unlimited in the following senses: he encompasses all logical possibilities, his "admirability" is unlimited in that his sensitivity to the feelings of other beings is complete,[22] he has an unlimited ability to preserve and harmonize values, and his "reliability" is unlimited in the sense that his intention to preserve and harmonize is absolutely fixed.[23]

Whitehead's "relative" God has two distinct natures—he calls them the Primordial Nature (exhibiting eternalistic traits) and the Consequent Nature (exhibiting temporalistic traits). Each dimension of this God supposedly contributes something to the growth and preservation of value. As Primordial, God is the repository of all eternal objects—by which Whitehead means all the qualities, characteristics, or properties that could characterize any event or set of events. However, God conceived as infinite in this sense is perfectly compatible with very limited power in manipulating actualities, and then such a God is no guarantee of the growth of value. So Whitehead must introduce something more than the infinitude of possibility. This guarantee, for Whitehead, amounts to the Primordial Nature's infinite capacity as final cause to present lures for novelty. It is assumed that the Primordial Nature's dangling of all possibilities before the world will eventually, by evoking novelty again and again, exhaust all the possibilities so that there will be a time when it can truly be said that God's infinity of possibilities has been realized. Whitehead calls the Primordial Nature the "Eros of the Universe"[24] and suggests that we

> must conceive the Divine Eros as the active entertainment of all ideals, with the urge to their finite realization, each in its due season. Thus a process must be inherent in God's nature, whereby his infinity is acquiring realization.[25]

The Consequent Nature of God, unlike the Primordial, is conscious. God is only conscious when his conceptual nature is fused with physical feeling. In addition to being conscious, God in his Consequent Nature is incomplete, everlasting (as distinct from eternal), and the conservator (with unlimited memory) and harmonizer of all actual value. God conserves and harmonizes in the following sense. Actual occasions replace each other in the stream of time. These actual occasions have freedom, and some evil is the inevitable result. What remains constant in the stream of time, however, is God, in his Consequent Nature, and in whose consciousness all the values that have ever been actualized are harmonized.

The nature of the value which the Consequent God supposedly harmonizes is an unusual one. God envisages all pure possibilities and desires their realization and consequently desires the realization of evil experiences, decisions and deeds, as well as indifferent or good ones. He clearly does not reject them but preserves "every actuality for what it can be in . . . a perfected system . . . woven by rightness of feeling into the harmony of the universal feeling."[26] Only by maximizing the potentialities of existence, both good and evil, can the greatest synthesis of value occur. However, the question arises: If God actually de-

sires the realization of evil potentialities, he cannot be said to
be, in any obvious sense of the word, unlimited in goodness.
Whitehead replies by reinterpreting ordinary notions of good
and evil. He asks us, as we shall see, to consider moral value
subordinate to aesthetic value.

While the Whitehead-Hartshorne variety of quasi-theism is
extremely interesting and important, it encounters certain difficulties which make ultimate success very unlikely.

(A) The distinction between God being "limited" versus
being "relative" seems spurious, not a real distinction at all.
One may say that God is only relative in the sense that natural
events do not thwart him but are the occasions for his exercise
of creative power; he still must admit that on his view of the
matter God is still limited in the sense that he neither creates
nor wholly controls actual occasions. Moreover, if God does not
wholly control actual occasions, it is difficult to see how there
is any real assurance of the growth of value. The two elements
of traditional theism reinforce each other. The unlimited power
of God insures the growth of value, and the latter requires the
notion of God's unlimited power. The mutual reinforcement,
however, is wholly lacking in Whitehead's system. The absence
points up a fundamental difficulty with his quasi-theism.

(B) There are serious difficulties with the Primordial Nature
of God as guarantor of the growth of value.

(i) The Primordial Nature guarantees something quite un-
exciting. It is able to guarantee the eventual appearance *serially*
of all value possibilities but not the eventual appearance *at one
time* of the maximum amount of value. It is as if someone told
you that he guaranteed that your family would have a million
dollars, and you found that he meant not that at some point
the family assets would be a million dollars but that a million
dollars would pass through the hands of the family in the course
of three generations.

Sometimes Whitehead seems to imply that the more exciting
sort of value growth is guaranteed, but surely the power necessary to make that guarantee is not derivable from the mere
presentation of possibilities to the world; and, as we shall see,
nothing in the Consequent Nature is in a position to do it either.

(ii) Moreover, the nature of what supposedly insures the realization of value is obscure and hardly personal enough to qualify Whitehead's view even as quasi-theistic. Sometimes Whitehead suggests that it is a principle, "The Principle of Concretion," that guarantees the realization of value.

> In the place of Aristotle's God as Prime Mover, we require God as the Principle of Concretion. . . . Eternal objects inform actual occasions with hierarchic patterns. . . . (E)very actual occasion is a limitation imposed on possibility, and . . . by virtue of this limitation the particular value of that shaped togetherness of things emerges.[27]

At other times he implies that Creativity guarantees it, but he takes pains to make us realize that creativity is not an entity.[28] Creativity is to be thought of as like Aristotelian matter, not having a character of its own.[29] Hence it seems that even if the guarantee is successful and is compatible with God's other limitations, it turns out that the guarantor *is not a being at all* but at best a principle. To have a theism of any kind there must be a *personal being* who is thought to guarantee the growth of value. Whatever it is that guarantees is considered worthy of worship, but here we are asked to worship a principle or a characterless stuff. This is theistic worship in a very loose sense indeed.

However, Whitehead frequently sees nothing untheistic about worship of such a principle. This principle is

> the actual but nontemporal entity whereby the indetermination of mere creativity is transmitted into a determinate freedom. This nontemporal actual entity is what men call God—the supreme God of rationalized religion.[30]

Every effort is made by both Whitehead and Hartshorne to make this principle share the attributes of a theistic God. Whitehead calls it an "actual but nontemporal entity." However, nothing is more puzzling about Whitehead than his describing the Primordial Nature as an entity after he has carefully constructed a monumental metaphysics in which all actual entities are considered becomings. He tries to avoid this glaring inconsistency by calling it a "nontemporal" entity but this only aggravates the problem because, in his metaphysics, all entities are to be understood in terms of process, and process necessarily involves time. He also tries to avoid the inconsistency by considering the Primordial Nature an entity "deficient in actuality" just as he considers eternal objects real and yet not actual. However, Whitehead's platonic difficulties are notorious, and surely any justification of his theism must be independent of his platonism.

Hartshorne announces that the Primordial Nature is "volitional," but it is obscure how something recognizable as will can be got out of a principle.[31] He calls the Primordial Nature "a supreme causal factor,"[32] but there are many causal factors that do not qualify as entities. If we say in dealing with a college administrator that his vanity is a factor to be reckoned with, we do not imply that his vanity is an object (entity) like a tusk protruding dangerously from his hide.

Whitehead suggests personality and entitativeness in the Primordial Nature by speaking of it as engaged in free action: "His unity of conceptual operations is a free creative act."[33] But this is to use *free, creative,* and *act* in ways utterly different from the ways he uses them in the rest of his philosophy. A "free creative act" elsewhere in his philosophy is a temporal process involving choice among possibilities by a particular subject experiencing the world from a particular perspective. Since the Primordial Nature is the collection of *all* possibilities, its coming to be cannot involve choice; since it is eternal, it cannot exclude any *possible* perspective.

In brief, the difficulty here is that insofar as one finds an infinite aspect of God compatible with his other limitations and capable of guaranteeing at least a serial realization of value, one has a God without personality and without even status as a distinct entity.

(C) Hartshorne thinks that the Consequent Nature of God is capable of guaranteeing the preservation of value because the Consequent Nature is infinite in at least this respect: He is capable of knowing and preserving without any loss (in all their immediacy) all past values.[34] The Consequent Nature is conscious (as the Primordial Nature is not) and all values that have ever been actual are harmonized in that consciousness. He is absolutely "admirable" in that his sensitivity to the feelings of others is unlimited. He is absolutely "reliable" in that nothing can make him waver from his intention to harmonize in his own consciousness.

However, this Consequent Nature is no more useful in guaranteeing anything about value than the Primordial Nature.

(i) Hartshorne's insistence on this power in God is inconsistent with his own (and Whitehead's) metaphysical principles according to which no actual entity can experience the immediacy of past (i.e., "objectively immortal") actual entities.[35] God, however, is an actual entity himself and yet is capable of an *infinite* amount of such experience.

(ii) But even if we assume that by some ontological miracle the Consequent Nature has infinite power to retain in immediacy all past values, what sort of triumph is that? Suppose that God occasionally has to wait one hundred years to find something worth saving. To be sure, God is doing a superb job of saving everything of value, but he is doing nothing to insure the growth of value or to insure that divine providence uses evil in the production of greater good, or that the good will outlast evil, and so on.

(iii) However, there remains a way, it is suggested, that the Consequent Nature can not only conserve value but actually promote it. The Consequent Nature acts indirectly by having its harmony felt by every individual,[36] and this felt harmony acts as an example which inspires them in their own efforts to promote harmony. But in Whitehead's own system this felt harmony is impossible. An individual (a society of actual entities) apprehends the past plainly and simply and is without any means of apprehending an "everlasting" harmony of past values formed in the divine mind. The impression that God can act in that way is created by a confusion between the past and the past as harmonized in the divine consciousness. Perhaps an example from outside Whiteheadian metaphysics would clarify this distinction. Two men may have witnessed the same series of events in a Nazi concentration camp and they now both remember them, but one (theodically inclined) has harmonized these events in his consciousness and the other has not so harmonized them. The two men apprehend the same past without the second man apprehending the first's harmonization and gaining inspiration thereby.

To sum up these difficulties in Whitehead's and Hartshorne's attempt to escape the dilemma, what little influence Whitehead's God has on the actual world (insuring continuous novelty), he has as a principle—not as a being or person. Insofar as God is a personal being, he is without any effect on the actual world (he only remembers and harmonizes in his own consciousness).

But now let us waive for the moment these objections and assume that Whitehead's God is both personal and able significantly, but indirectly, to affect the actual world. Whitehead's God might be said to affect indirectly the actual world by giving each actual occasion an initial aim which it can freely modify. God could then be said to *persuade* but not to coerce. God guarantees the growth of value only if there is widespread human cooperation, and this cooperation is dependent on men being persuaded, not coerced, to cooperate with God. This guarantee might be called a conditional guarantee. It could then be contrasted with the unconditional guarantee of more traditional theism where the triumph of good is guaranteed *regardless* of what men do. The Whiteheadian is suggesting that, although a conditional guarantee is a necessary part of theism, it is a serious mistake to suppose, as many have in the past, that an *un*conditional guarantee is necessary to theism.

What we wish to argue is that the conditional guarantee in the end encounters difficulties just as serious as those encountered by the unconditional guarantee that has been abandoned. Consider the following analogy. An especially effective leader of an organization might be described as someone who is powerful enough to guarantee the success of the organization *if* most of the members pitch in and help. If they choose not to cooperate, the leader's best efforts will not insure success. One can be sure that the leader will exercise his great powers of persuasion, but if the members refuse to cooperate, his best efforts will be in vain. The leader, like God, can offer only a conditional guarantee of success. Such a qualified reassurance, it is argued, is the only sort of guarantee logically compatible with a genuine respect for human freedom. However, there are two fundamental difficulties with this aspect of the White-headian view. First, if cases can be found in which there has been widespread human cooperation and yet there has been no success, these cases would count as evidence against the existence of such a conditional guarantee. Such cases seem easy to find. Second, the process theist also will have difficulty in making the *amount* of evil in the world compatible with great persuasive power. In our analogy, if a large number of the members of the organization regularly do evil, we begin to suspect that the leader is not very persuasive. A leader may be trying very hard to be persuasive, but if people are seldom persuaded, surely this indicates that he lacks persuasive power. How can one measure persuasive power except by seeing how often people are persuaded? How can the process theist show that the *amount* of uncooperativeness in the world is compatible with the unlimited persuasive power of God? To be sure, the process theist has avoided the incompatibilities created by the idea of coercive power, but it seems that he will have much the same problem with the incompatibilities created by per-suasive power. It is a little too convenient simply to attribute all the growth to God's persuasive power and all the evil to the world's refusal to be persuaded.

In fact, the appeal to persuasive power appears to be simply a process form of the classical free-will solution and closely related to John Hick's discussion of the development of "authentic fiduciary attitudes"—both of which we have previously criticized in detail.

(D) Let us waive all the above difficulties with Whitehead's version of quasi-theism. Let us now assume that the guarantee is successful and consider in some detail the nature of the evil controlled and the value guaranteed. Here the worst deficiencies of all arise.

Evil, Whitehead sometimes suggests, is simply loss of imme-diacy.

The ultimate evil in the temporal world is deeper than any specific evil. It lies in the fact that the past fades, that time is a 'perpetual perishing.'[37]

This is an odd understanding of evil indeed. Suppose Smith were to say to his friend Jones that he is not concerned with his present pains because he is gifted with an extraordinary memory, remembers all his friend's past experiences, and will include them all harmoniously in his own consciousness, without the slightest loss of immediacy. We doubt that Jones would be impressed by his friend's statement that the only genuine evil is loss of immediacy, and so what he supposes to be evil is good insofar as it has immediacy that can be harmoniously preserved. We would understand Jones' growing feeling that Smith is something less than a true friend. What Jones wishes to know is why the immediacy initially has to be so painful to him. Could not such a harmony be achieved with less painful immediacy?

Whitehead sometimes seems to say that there simply isn't such a thing as physical or moral evil independent of aesthetic value. "All order is therefore aesthetic order; and the moral order is merely certain aspects of aesthetic order."[38] Therefore what appears as gratuitous evil is really just the makings of aesthetic value in the Consequent Nature. However, Whitehead in this case must do more than say that good is the preservation of immediacy because no one will accept that as an alternative theory of value.

On the positive side, Whitehead suggests that value is to be measured by the "massiveness" and "intensity" of experience.

> . . . the parts contribute to the massive feeling of the whole, and the whole contributes to the intensity of feeling of the parts. Thus the subjective forms of these prehensions are severally and jointly interwoven in patterned contrasts.[39]

It may be protested that, for the aesthetic gain, it is not necessary to have all the physical evil in the world. Surely many earthquakes, for example, could be eliminated without a sacrifice of aesthetic value. The objector here is, in effect, accusing Whitehead's God (with his concern for only aesthetic value) of being not all good as a theistic God should be. Certainly a God who is willing to pay any amount in moral and physical evil to gain aesthetic value is an unlovable being.

> The real world is good when it is beautiful. . . . Of course it is true that the defence of morals is the battle-cry which best rallies stupidity against change. Perhaps countless ages ago respectable amoebae refused to migrate from ocean to dry land—refusing in defence of morals.[40]

Surely many would want to side with the amoebae.

Another tack taken by Whitehead is to argue that evil in the world is what makes possible novelty and the avoidance of "the tameness of outworn perfection."

> . . . the contribution to Beauty which can be supplied by Discord— in itself destructive and evil—is the positive feeling of a quick shift of aim from the tameness of outworn perfection to some other ideal with its freshness still upon it.[41]

Here the problem is not God's *power* to insure the growth of value but his *goodness*. Even if God has the power to insure the ultimate triumph of an end of his choice, it is merely an aesthetic end; God seems to lack goodness in that he is not concerned about the cost in human feeling. Hartshorne is inclined to defend Whitehead by saying that God is a fellow sufferer.[42] He experiences all the pain of beings in the world *as his own*. He is absolutely "admirable" because he is absolutely sensitive to the feeling of others. It is implied that, if God is a fellow sufferer, he cannot be accused of selfishly sacrificing human feeling to his own ends. His goodness *in the sense of selflessness* is protected. But it can still be objected that a being who sacrifices human feeling to aesthetic ends, however selflessly, is not totally good. Suppose a human being were selflessly to torture himself (and some of his friends) in the interest of aesthetic value. He would surely not be considered a completely good individual, although of course he would be considered good in one respect, namely, selflessness.

Apart from the objection that God's goodness would be limited to selflessness, there is still the objection that God must be very weak indeed if he is unable to move toward an aesthetic end without an enormous cost in pain (his own and that of others); he is apparently so weak that he cannot guarantee his own welfare. If he is that weak, obviously he is not able, as a theistic God should be, to *insure* the ultimate triumph of an end of his choice, although of course he can *try* with absolute "reliability." It is possible for a tennis novice to try with *absolute reliability* to beat the world champion, but no one confuses reliability of intention with reliability of success in that case.

(E) Worse still, Whitehead's God is not only lacking power to move the world inexorably toward a goal of his choice, but he is also lacking the power merely to jam the mechanism of creation. God may not have created the world but he has been "with creation" from the very beginning and presumably recognized his limitations very early. Given initial situations, the best of what is possible is sometimes ghastly, and surely God must have been powerful enough to "call the whole thing off" even if not in a position to create and change the world as he liked. It takes a skilled mechanic to assemble an automobile engine but only a small child to put it out of order. Indeed, if God is so paralyzed that he is unable to jam the mechanism of creation, he should at least regret that nothing better was possible instead of rejoicing in the maximum of value that he alone can experience.

(F) Finally, Whitehead may insist that ultimately there is nothing to regret since something is better than nothing! Here he would fall back on his aesthetic theory of value according to which value is equated with "vivid experience" or "definiteness."[43] Naturally, any world will have more "vivid experiences" than no world since there is no such thing as negative vividness, as there is of negative moral value. Of course this strategy would merely reintroduce all the problems connected with the use of aesthetic value in solving the problem of moral and physical evil.

VI

Josiah Royce, like other quasi-theists, is unsatisfied with traditional solutions of the problem of evil. He thinks that the problem can be solved only by modifying the conception of God in such a way that the traits creating the problem are removed without eliminating the traits that make possible theistic worship. He finds that only the metaphysics of absolute idealism make possible such a modification. Those who have relied on other metaphysics have been in difficulty, according to Royce, because they insist that God as creator must be separate from the world. If God is instead considered a creator in the sense of an Absolute within which there is a finite world, there is no problem of evil. It can no longer be said that evil in the world should have been prevented by an omnipotent, all-good God because that evil is now considered a part of God; as a part of the Absolute, it is not isolated but rather contributes to the eternal perfection. "For an idealistic theory of Being this very presence of ill in the temporal order is the condition of the eternal order."[44] If one considers evil as integral to God, it is no longer a problem. God is all-powerful and all-good and uses with complete effectiveness finite evil to the end of his eternal harmony.

However, it seems that an Absolute that contains evil cannot be all-good as a theistic God must be. Royce's answer follows.

> When I experience the victory of moral insight over the bad will, I experience in one indivisible moment both the partial evil of the selfish impulse (which in itself as a separate fact would be wholly bad) and the universal good of the moral victory. . . . And what we here experience in the single moment of time, and in the narrowness of our finite lives, God must experience and eternally . . .[45]

God, in short, cannot be wholly good *unless* he has evil within himself to triumph over.

Such an all-inclusive, abstract Absolute in which evil plays an integral part does not appear to be the personal God of theism, but Royce insists that his conception of God is "distinctly theistic, and not pantheistic."[46] God is not a mere abstraction but is a will, although not the will of a being separate from the world.

> The Divine Will is simply *that aspect of the Absolute which is expressed in the concrete and differentiated individuality of the world.*[47]

This factor, the Will, individuates both the Absolute and its world. Hereby the Absolute becomes a Person.[48]

God's personal will is genuinely expressed in the individuality of the world. Such an all-inclusive personal will would seem to imply that individual human beings have no genuine reality except as part of the "World-Self" and consequently that the problem of evil has been solved at the cost of human individuality.

To this Royce answers that the metaphysics of absolute idealism shows us that an individual is only a genuine individual insofar as he is part of the Absolute.

> You are unique and therefore individual in your life and meaning, just because you have your place in the divine life, and that life is one. We finite beings then are unique and individual in our differences, from one another and from all possible beings, just because we share in the very uniqueness of God's individuality and purpose.[49]

Although Royce seriously grapples with the problem and clearly recognizes the failures of earlier attempts to deal with it, his own approach encounters a number of difficulties.

(A) God as the Absolute can hardly be considered the creator of the world in the traditional theistic sense. A theistic God must *cause* the world to come into being; he must be First Cause. Yet Royce says that "the conception of causation does not apply to the whole of reality."[50] If one considers God, Royce argues, "the whole of reality," one cannot expect him to create anything, since anything existent would already be part of him, that is, part of "the [eternal] whole of reality." One certainly cannot speak meaningfully of the whole of reality being created by anything prior to it because that prior being would have to be itself part of reality. By construing God as the whole of reality, one eliminates the *ordinary* notion of creation altogether.

In the ordinary theistic view, reality is divided into supernatural, uncreated being and natural, created being. The first part of reality creates the second part. "The whole of reality" does not act in any way but is simply the sum of the supernatural and natural reality.

Nonetheless, Royce wants to avoid the complete elimination

of the notion of creation because that would leave him open to the charge that he is defending not theism, but pantheism. He speaks of the "World-Creator," and seems to be suggesting that the Absolute be considered a creator in the sense that any organic whole creates its parts.[51] A part's existence is dependent on the existence of the whole and so, in a sense, it can be said that the part's existence is brought about by the whole. If one thinks, as absolute idealists do, of the Absolute as an *organic* whole in which all the parts are interdependent, one can understand how it can be suggested that the finite world is dependent upon the Absolute for its existence and so, in a sense, is created by the Absolute. For Royce *being created* is synonymous with *being part of an organic whole.* Not only is this an odd notion of creation, but it is a notion that is drastically in conflict with theism's insistance on considering God the only being capable, strictly speaking, of creating anything. On Royce's view creation becomes commonplace. Any organic whole is capable of it, and it is merely a matter of the degree of inclusiveness of the particular whole. For the genuine theist divine creation is *different in kind* from natural creation.

(B) God as the Absolute is not personal as a genuinely theistic God is. This has been pointed out by other absolute idealists such as F. H. Bradley, but Royce persistently disagreed with them.

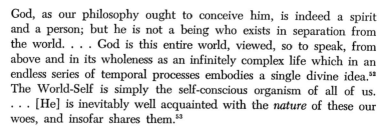

> God, as our philosophy ought to conceive him, is indeed a spirit and a person; but he is not a being who exists in separation from the world. . . . God is this entire world, viewed, so to speak, from above and in its wholeness as an infinitely complex life which in an endless series of temporal processes embodies a single divine idea.[52] The World-Self is simply the self-conscious organism of all of us. . . . [He] is inevitably well acquainted with the *nature* of these our woes, and insofar shares them.[53]

Even if one accepts the metaphysics of absolute idealism and its belief that reality is an organic whole, there is no reason to suppose that that organic whole is personal. Some organic wholes are associated with persons and some not. One can enthusiastically look at the world "in it wholeness" without finding anything personal in that wholeness.

Royce suggests that the Absolute is personal to its parts in that it is naturally familiar with "our woes" which are, after all, necessarily part of itself. Surely, however, mere organic *inclusion* is not the same as sympathy. We need only point out that there are functionally complex and "organic" social organizations in which the society (taken as a higher type of individual) is not considered in any way personal and *a fortiori* not thought to feel sympathy for its members. There is, indeed, every reason to believe that the bigger the society the *less* personal the organic whole. We would expect Royce's Absolute Community to be absolutely *im*personal.

What gave as sophisticated a philosopher as Royce his confidence that the Absolute is personal? There are certain elements in Royce's metaphysics that gave him this confidence. He first proves the existence of absolute truth. Second he proves that the existence of absolute truth entails the existence of a knower of this truth. He then argues that omniscience entails all the other omni-traits of a theistic God.[54] Apart from the great difficulties in proving the existence of absolute truth and its entailment of an omniscient being, it is odd (for anyone but an idealist) to suppose that absolute knowledge must be resident in a personal being who will answer prayers.[55] Although staunch rationalists may overlook it, there is a vast difference between knowing precisely what suffering is going on (e.g., in a gas chamber) and being sympathetic with the individual sufferer. One could much more easily imagine such an absolute knower as a vast computor calculating with infinite accuracy the possible contributions to be made by each thing in the world to the welfare of the computor.

(C) Even if the Absolute is granted to be genuinely creative and personal, Royce does not succeed in showing that he is absolved of responsibility for evil. Royce thinks that

> the answer to Job is: God is not in ultimate essence another being than yourself. He is the Absolute Being. . . . When you suffer, your sufferings are God's sufferings. . . . (T)he true question then is: Why does God thus suffer?[56]

If reality is an organic whole, evil and everything else can only be understood in the context of reality as a whole. The problem of evil, Royce suggests, is caused by bad metaphysics in which the organic character of reality is not recognized and God is thought of as a separate being. Once monistic idealism is accepted, the question is merely one of how the evil is justified as contributing to the eternal perfection of the Absolute.[57]

> As the evil impulse is to the good man, so is the evil will of the wicked man to the life of God, in which he is an element. . . . Goodness as a moral experience is for us the overcoming of experienced evil; and in the eternal life of God the realization of goodness must have the same sort of organic relation to evil as it has in us.[58]

This appears to be a form of the traditional character-building argument we have criticized in a previous chapter. The difference is that here it is God's character that is being built.

The appeal to the building of God's character seems at first superfluous. It would seem that if Royce believes that evil can be justified in terms of character building, he would appeal to human character building without bringing in what to many may appear an outrageous slur on God's character. Royce feels compelled to introduce divine character building because he candidly admits that "much evil exists whose use as a means we cannot even faintly conceive."[59] Royce's procedure is simply to justify what evil he can in terms of human character building and then justify whatever evil remains in terms of divine character building. He holds that some evil is gratuitous relative to *human* character building but no evil is gratuitous to the Absolute.

Unfortunately, the divine form of the character-building argument works even less well than the human form. There is at least some plausibility in justifying some evil in terms of human character building; the glaring difficulty is faced only when one asks why there is so much evil. But it is very odd to suggest that God's character needs building. If God's character needs building, then he is not all-good. It causes difficulties to limit God's power as Brightman and others do, but it is far more embarrassing to suggest he has a weak moral will that needs to be strengthened in a struggle to overcome the evils of the world.

But even if we assume that a theistic God's character can need strengthening, Royce gives us no assurance that: (i) it is possible for God to overcome the evils and not to become defeated or depraved as many men do in the face of evil, and (ii) the evils that exist serve this character-building purpose with maximum economy.

(D) Howard Jefferson and others have rightly protested that even if the divine character-building argument were to solve the problem for the Absolute, it suggests that the Absolute is rather indifferent in his attitude toward the values of human beings.[60] Royce tries to use the metaphysics of absolute idealism in which the Absolute and the individual are inseparable to deal with this difficulty also. He assures suffering human beings that the divine triumph can be shared by all,[61] and that God and the individual are so metaphysically inseparable that an individual's pain can be relieved by his direct experience of God's triumph.[62] Of course we all understand what it is in a painful situation to derive vicarious satisfaction from someone else's triumph, and this understanding is what makes Royce's answer seem plausible. But Royce himself seems to realize that such vicarious satisfaction in the triumph of a being distinct from oneself is usually very limited in its power to compensate for one's pain. Often human beings make every effort to relieve their pain by vicarious satisfaction and fail. Accordingly Royce suggests that it is not merely a vicarious experiencing of triumph but an experience of one's own triumph since the individual is inseparable from the Absolute.

This strategy causes as many problems as it solves. Insofar as the individual's and the Absolute's experience are one, the evil—as it is experienced by the individual, and, indeed, the individual's very personal identity—is illusory. And, as we noted earlier, Royce emphatically rejects the solution according to which evil is an illusion.

(E) Finally, Royce fails to show why this solution of the problem of evil does not discourage moral effort. Royce obviously recognizes this difficulty in the other solutions of the problem of evil which explicitly rely on a claim that evil is an illusion.[63] But he thinks that in his solution there is "a moral order which is . . . at once divine in its perfection so that we can worship it and great in its needs so that our life may not be vain as we try to serve the good."[64] However, it is not clear why someone should make an effort to remove evil in himself or in the world if God has unlimited power to use that evil to build his own character.

In traditional theism it is said that God is eternally perfect while the world is imperfect. Individual human beings cannot do anything to improve God but they can do something to improve the world. But if as in Royce's metaphysics, God and the world are eternally one perfect organic whole, there is no reason for an individual to make a moral effort, except perhaps to do evil so that God may have more on which to build his character. This is another case in which a quasi-theist in straining to solve the problem of evil unavoidably eliminates important features of theistic belief. The final result is a conception of God that *neither* absolves God of responsibility for evil *nor* serves as a genuine theism, and the quasi-theist is worse off than ever.

VII

One quasi-theist has remarked that "all simplifications of religious dogma are shipwrecked upon the rock of the problem of evil." The point of our final chapter has been to show that the same can be said of more complicated dogmas.[65] When the fog lifts, the "rock" turns out to be part of the mainland.

NOTES

1. Charles Hartshorne and William L. Reese: *Philosophers Speak of God.* Chicago, University of Chicago Press, 1953, p. 16.
2. *Creative Evolution,* translated by A. Mitchell, New York, Random House, Modern Library, 1944, p. 271.
3. Selections in Hartshorne and Reese, *op. cit.,* pp. 396-404.
4. *Agapology: The Rational Love-Philosophy Guide of Life.* Boston, Christopher Publishing House, 1965, pp. 31-68.
5. *Behind the Universe: A Doctor's Religion.* New York, Harper & Brothers, 1943, pp. 290-303.
6. *The Way of Things.* New York, Prentice-Hall, 1940, pp. 482-539.

7. Josiah Royce, *et al.: Conception of God.* New York, The Macmillan Company, 1897, pp. 67-78.
8. *Space, Time and Deity.* New York, Dover Publications, 1966, vol. II, Book IV.
9. We can hardly begin to describe all the varieties of quasi-theism and their difficulties, but before we go on to consider the most plausible quasi-theisms, we must point out one especially vicious fault to be found in some of the most spectacular pantheistic conceptions of God. In these philosophies we are told that we need not worry about God's goodness so long as we are confident of him as the controlling force in the cosmos. Supreme power, they appear to hold, is its own justification. These thinkers, unfortunately, fail to appreciate the repugnant moral consequences of this view.

Typically these philosophers start by speculating on the basis of physical sciences, as to what is the most powerful law in the cosmos. Having found such a law (with evidence satisfactory to them if to no one else), they tell us that it is God. To questions about the divinity of such an almighty cosmological law they reply that surely one cannot doubt the value of such a God, since all value is dependent on this most powerful physical law controlling the cosmos. If all is dependent on it, they insist, one can hardly suppose that it is not good. It is here that the dangerous fallacy lies. From the fact that to achieve valuable ends one must take account of whatever supreme powers there are, it does not follow that those supreme powers are good.

Perhaps the fallacy will become clear in a political analogy. Suppose we are in Germany in the 1930's. Someone, ordinarily benign, says that, after considerable thought, he has become dedicated to Hitler. We are dismayed and ask for an explanation. Our friend says that it is quite simple; he has studied contemporary Germany and found that without a doubt Hitler is the most powerful force in the country; to get anything done one must take account of Hitler and his aims. We are amazed at his assumption that naked power, if it is great enough, is its own justification. We suggest that the fact that one must take account of the Nazis in order to be able to do anything of value does not show that we must think the Nazi aims have value. Under the circumstances the individual with moral integrity presumably would make it his business to know what Hitler's aims and methods are *in order to thwart them most effectively* and to achieve the ends he himself has; he does not worship the supreme power of Hitler as its own justification. Similarly, in speaking of God one can rightly insist that we should make it our business to know precisely what laws are supreme in the cosmos without insisting that such a law be worshipped *unless the operation of the law happens to tend to move the cosmos in a direction which coincides with our own* (of course worship of even such a principle would be dubious because of its impersonality). If the law does not move things toward our ends, we are obliged to do our best to thwart the tendency.

Those who propose conceptions of God requiring worship of sheer cosmological power often fancy that they have adopted a strikingly original religious outlook. In fact, their view is nothing more than a pantheistic form of Calvinism. To be in awe of God's power was sufficient for the Calvinists as it is for them. In one view, one is in awe of the naked power of a spiritual being, and in the other it is awe of the naked power of a physical law that is advocated; the hideous moral consequences are the same. The only other differences are that in the pantheistic version one is in a better position precisely to predict the hideous acts of God and one can be confident that God is not being *intentionally* unjust in his distribution of suffering.

10. Edgar Sheffield Brightman: *A Philosophy of Religion,* New York, Prentice-Hall, 1940; *The Problem of God,* New York, The Abingdon Press, 1930; "The Given and Its Critics," *Religion in Life,* I, 134-45, 1932. Roland Stahl: "Professor Brightman's Theory of the Given," *Religion in Life,* XXIII:537-48, 1954. Andrew Banning, "Professor Brightman's Theory of a Limited God: A Criticism," *Harvard Theological Review,* XXVII:145-68, 1934. Peter Anthony Bertocci, *Introduction to the Philosophy of Religion,* Englewood Cliffs, Prentice-Hall, 1951.

11. *A Philosophy of Religion,* p. 316.

12. *Problem of God,* p. 122.

13. "The Given and Its Critics," p. 135.

14. *Problem of God,* p. 187.

15. *Ibid.,* p. 137.

16. *Ibid.,* pp. 179-80.

17. Stahl, *op. cit.,* p. 541.

18. *Problem of God,* p. 11.

19. *A Philosophy of Religion,* p. 328.

20. In a recent paper Hartshorne has diverged from Whitehead ["A New Look at the Problem of Evil," in Frederick C. Dommeyer (Ed.), *Current Philosophical Issues: Essays in Honor of Curt John Ducasse,* Springfield, Charles C. Thomas, 1966, pp. 201-212]. He simplifies his solution to the problem of evil by limiting it to a panpsychical version of the free-will solution. This sort of free-will solution has been used before by Macintosh [Cf. Vergilius Ferm (Ed.), *Encyclopedia of Religion,* Paterson, Littlefield, Adams, 1959 paperback edition, p. 264]. The criticisms we have made of the free-will solution in Chapter Four would also apply here.

21. This is Hartshorne's term for Whitehead's idea. See Charles Hartshorne,

The Divine Relativity, New Haven, Yale University Press, 1964; chapters I and II are entitled "God as Supreme, Yet Indebted to All" and "God as Supreme, Yet Related to All."

22. *Ibid.*, pp. 42-47.
23. *Ibid.*, pp. 22-24.
24. *Adventures of Ideas.* Cambridge, U. P., 1942, p. 326.
25. *Ibid.*, p. 357.
26. *Process and Reality.* Cambridge, U. P., 1929, p. 489.
27. *Science and the Modern World.* Cambridge, U. P., 1932, p. 216.
28. *Religion in the Making.* New York, The Macmillan Co., 1926, p. 92.
29. J. S. Bixler in P. A. Schilpp (Ed.): *The Philosophy of Alfred North Whitehead.* New York, Tudor Publishing Co., 1951, p. 493.
30. *Religion in the Making*, p. 90.
31. P. A. Schilpp (Ed.): *The Philosophy of Alfred North Whitehead*, p. 530.
32. *Ibid.*, p. 517.
33. *Process and Reality*, p. 487.
34. *Man's Vision of God.* New York, Harper & Brothers, 1941, p. 239.
35. Cf. *Modes of Thought.* New York, The Macmillan Co., 1938, p. 131.
36. Daniel Day Williams: "How Does God Act? An Essay in Whitehead's Metaphysics," in William L. Resse and Eugene Freeman (Eds.): *The Hartshorne Festschrift: Process and Divinity*, LaSalle, Open Court Publishing Co., 1964, p. 179.
37. *Process and Reality*, p. 482.
38. *Religion in the Making*, p. 105.
39. *Adventures of Ideas*, pp. 324-325.
40. *Ibid.*, pp. 345-346.
41. *Ibid.*, pp. 330-331.
42. *The Logic of Perfection.* LaSalle, Open Court Publishing Co., 1962, p. 44. Also in Schilpp (Ed.): *The Philosophy of Alfred North Whitehead*, p. 553.
43. *Religion in the Making*, p. 113.
44. Josiah Royce: *The World and the Individual.* New York, The Macmillan Company, 1904, vol. II, p. 385.
45. *The Religious Aspect of Philosophy.* New York, Harper Torchbook, 1958, pp. 452-53.
46. *The Conception of God*, pp. 49-50.
47. *Ibid.*, p. 202.
48. *Ibid.*, p. 349.
49. *The Conception of Immortality.* Boston, Houghton, Mifflin, 1900, p. 68.
50. *The Conception of God*, p. 203.
51. *Ibid.*, p. 203.
52. *William James and Other Essays.* New York, The Macmillan Company, 1912, pp. 167-68.

53. *The Spirit of Modern Philosophy.* Boston, Houghton, Mifflin, 1892, p. 437.
54. *The Conception of God,* pp. 7-8.
55. *Studies in Good and Evil.* Hamden, Archon Books, 1964, p. 24.
56. *Studies in Good and Evil,* p. 14.
57. *Ibid.,* p. 17; *The World and the Individual,* vol. II, p. 396.
58. *The Religious Aspect of Philosophy,* pp. 455-56.
59. *Ibid.,* p. 267.
60. Howard Jefferson, "Royce on the Problem of Evil," *Journal of Religion,* 1931.
61. *Spirit of Modern Philosophy,* p. 460.
62. *Ibid.,* pp. 470-71.
63. *The World and the Individual,* vol. II, p. 397.
64. *Spirit of Modern Philosophy,* p. 454.
65. Another complicated quasi-theism has been advanced recently by Pierre Teilhard de Chardin. *The Phenomenon of Man,* New York, Harper, 1959, is his most widely read book. Teilhard argues for a temporalistic pantheism in which evolution is seen as moving toward "the Omega point." Eventually, he says, "hatred and internecine struggles will have disappeared in the ever-warmer radiance of Omega" (*Ibid.,* p. 288). From this evolutionary movement he argues that Omega is an already existing deity because it could not "exercise this action were it not in sort loving and lovable *at this very moment*" (*Ibid.,* p. 269). Clearly Teilhard has as much difficulty in construing this evolutionary direction as a personal being as Whitehead has in construing the Primordial Nature as a being. Among the many other difficulties he shares with Whitehead are those associated with the reinterpretation of value. For example, Teilhard's reinterpretation of love as "psychical convergence" (*Ibid.,* p. 265) is parallel to Whitehead's appeal to aesthetic value. Even if we assume the empirical truth of their evolutionary cosmologies and can bring ourselves to worship such unusual values, both philosophers fail to take seriously the unnecessary cost of the realization of these values in human suffering. Teilhard, like Whitehead, must show that *all* the evil in the world is genuinely necessary to the achievement of this end and that no alternative evolutionary process usable by a very powerful being could have achieved this end at *less* cost.

INDEX

A

Absolute, the: in Royce, 125-132

Aesthetic view of evil: as a version of the ultimate harmony solution, 69; in Whitehead and Hartshorne, 123-25

Afterlife, or spa argument: 65

Aldrich, Virgil: on God as personal, 19

Alexander, Samuel: as quasi-theist, 10, 106-107

All or nothing fallacy: in Hick's theodicy, 84-90

All's well in God's view: as version of ultimate harmony solution, 15, 60-62

All's well that ends well: as version of ultimate harmony solution, 63-65

Altizer, Thomas J. J.: as influenced by Tillich's quasi-theism, 36

Animal pain: and the by-product solution, 55-56

Anselm, Saint: God as a metaphysical necessity, 47

Augustine, Saint: his view of evil as privation of good, 4-5, 65-66, 79; as opposed to theological voluntarism, 44-45; his aesthetic view of evil in Descartes' thought, 76

Austin, J. L.: his influence on linguistic theology, 20, 35

B

Banning, Andrew: on Brightman, 134

Barth, Karl: as evasionist, 7, 20-21, 23-25, 35; as both evasionist and quasi-theist, 11; his theory of *Das Nichtige,* 18

Belief in God: as opposed to belief in the existence of God, 7, 25-26

Bergson, Henri: as quasi-theist, 10, 106

Berman, Louis: as quasi-theist, 10, 106

Bertocci, Peter, 134

Bixler, J. S.: on Whitehead, 135

Bradley, F. H.: compared to Ramsey, 101, 103; and Royce, 128

Brightman, Edgar S.: his quasi-theism, 10-11, 107-14, 134

Brown, Patterson: as denier of problem, 42-46, 51

Buttrick, George A.: his use of the Event of Christ's life, 72-74, 80

C

Campbell, Keith: his criticism of Patterson Brown's denial, 46, 51

Character-building solution: 69-70; Hick's use of, 83-90; Royce's divine form of, 130

Christ: his life as a solution, according to Buttrick, 72-74

Circle, theological: 7, 21-23, 26-28

Coles, Robert: his report of a Negro child's view of evil, 79

Communication, between God and man: in Hick, 85-86; in Brightman, 113-14; in Whitehead and Hartshorne, 121-22

Compassion: evil necessary for, 60, 79, 88-89

Concretion, the principle of: in Whitehead, 118

Contrast: evil necessary for, 53-54

Creation: in Brightman, 109; in Royce, 127-28

Creativity: in Tillich, 29; in Bergson, 106; in Whitehead, 118

137

DATE DUE

OC 31 '68		
JA 13 '69		
FEB 11 1969	RESERVED	
305, 306		
FEB 21 9 P.M.		
MAR 26 9 P.M.		
APR 14 1969. 9 AM		
2 P.M.		
APR 30 9 P.M.		
MAY 1 9 A.M.		
MAY 1 2 P.M.		
	JAN 2 3 1974	
NO 13 '69	MAY 1 5 1974	
FE 2 '70	MAR 2 9 1976	
MY 6 '70	JAN 2 7 1993	
MR 20 '71		
DEC 21 1972		
APR 1 5 1973		
GAYLORD		PRINTED IN U.S.A.